A FRAGILE KINGDOM

Reflections on Sunday Readings

To Briege —
thankyou for your kindness
Philomene.

Gary Wade

First published 2005 by
Veritas Publications
7/8 Lower Abbey Street
Dublin 1, Ireland
Email publications@veritas.ie
Website www.veritas.ie

ISBN 1 85390 925 4

Designed and Typeset by Paula Ryan
Printed in the Republic of Ireland by Betaprint, Dublin

The fresco used on the front cover shows 'St Francis Giving his Mantle to a Poor Man' by Giotto and is reproduced courtesy of the Upper Church of St Francis in Assisi.

Quotations from W.B. Yeats' 'The Second Coming' on pg 13 and 'The Stolen Child' on pg 24 are reprinted courtesy of the AP Watt literary estate. Quotation from Louis McNeice's 'Cradle Song for Eleanor' on pg 31 from *Selected Poems* (Faber & Faber, 1998) used with permission. Quotation from W.H. Auden's 'The Shield of Achilles' from *Scanning the Century: The Penguin Book of the Twentieth Century in Poetry* (Viking, 1999). Quotation from Brian Friel's 'The Diviner' from *Selected Stories* (Gallery Press, 1979) used with permission. 'To A Child' by Patrick Kavanagh on pg 106 is reproduced with kind permission of the Jonathan Williams literary agency. Extract from Seamus Heaney's translation of Sophocles' *Philoctetes* on pg 124 (Farrar, Straus and Giroux, 1991).

CONTENTS

To my parents,
my first teachers in the faith

ACKNOWLEDGEMENTS

I wish to acknowledge all who encouraged me to write this book. In particular I owe a deep debt of gratitude to the people of Holy Family parish, Derry City, for their inspiration and energy which nurtured these reflections. I thank the pupils and staff of Saint Columb's College, my home for the last eight years, for forgiving my weaknesses and strengthening my faith. I thank Father Eamon Martin, my companion and colleague, for his generous advice and wise counsel. I also wish to thank Father Patrick O'Kane and Father John R. Walsh for their unstinting friendship and their encouragement to undertake this project. I am grateful to Mr Sean McMahon who offered me invaluable and professional advice, most graciously, at the very first stages of the manuscript.

Finally I acknowledge all the staff at Veritas Publications, without whom this project could never have reached completion. It has been a pleasure working with and learning from people of such professional expertise.

PREFACE

The ideas for the reflections that follow were generated by various Sundays and Feasts in the Liturgical Year, covering the three-year cycle. They have been written, however, as reflections on Christian living and, therefore, do not follow any particular cycle or liturgical sequence. In arranging them I have attempted to invite the reader to move from despair to hope, from the fragments of our faith and our lives to their restoration through the Risen Christ. At this point I beg the readers' patience. Since the reflections in the first two sections concentrate on brokenness in both the Church and society some readers may find them hard work. Although the series of reflections begins on a note of despair and ends on a more hopeful note, it is not necessary to read them in this way. The reader can dip in and out of the series without having to pay detailed attention to the overall theme of the book.

I have attempted in this book to order my own thought and to articulate for myself, as well as my readers, the joys and challenges of living the Christian life in today's Church and society. Much of this book is personal and I share it with you in the hope that you will connect with some of the very human stories I recall. It is also personal in the sense that I have been awakened to the great gift of God's grace in the world, not only in the human encounters I have been part of, but also in the expression of life's meaning and value in literature and in art.

So these reflections often jump from very real human encounters to drawing out the moral significance of a novel or the spiritual insight of a particular painter or sculptor. It is hoped in this way to show that God's grace can be revealed in many different ways and that the Kingdom of God is present in many different aspects of life. Above all I have tried to articulate the fragility of life and of faith and the necessity of treating each other with compassion and kindness, aware that the Kingdom of God is with us and still in the future. We live out our lives in faith, hope and love in this fragile kingdom.

A FRAGILE KINGDOM

The thread running through this series of reflections is the fragile nature of the kingdom of God, the kingdom present in the here and now and the kingdom we await in the future. I begin deliberately with Giotto's frescoes in the Basilica of St Francis in Assisi as an image or a symbol of the kingdom of God. Giotto, born about 1266, is widely recognised as the first great artist of the early Italian Renaissance. His frescoes are among some of the most beautiful paintings in the world. They are the earliest works attributed to the artist. The frescoes' simple but magnificent beauty might reveal something of God's kingdom to us, something of the beauty of living in God's presence. But their fall in 1997, as a result of an earthquake, reminds us too of the fragile nature of the kingdom, of our responsibility to preserve God's kingdom in the fragmented world in which we live. Our broken humanity, our weakness, the fissures that separate us from each other and from God are reflected in the broken fragments of Giotto's frescoes as they lay on the floor of the Basilica in the aftermath of that tragedy. The slow and loving process by which art restorers began the work of piecing them together over a period of five years might equally become the metaphor for our own redemption, piecing together the fragments of our lives through faith in the salvation Christ has won for us. So that experience of the frescoes in terms of creation, fall and redemption becomes for me a living metaphor of how I experience the kingdom of God in my own life and in the life of the Church.

If I apply that metaphor to the Church and the society in which we live and through which we experience the kingdom of God then it is clear that we experience the kingdom in-between creation and redemption, between its presence and its full realisation at the end of time. The image of the damaged and fragmented frescoes becomes real again in the fragmented Church and society in which we live. For at least the last ten years the Church has become destabilised by the revelations and immense hurt caused by child sexual abuse. Even in the early nineties when I was a student for the priesthood one could not have foreseen the extent to which the Church would be changed, both for the better and for the worse, in the course of the next ten years. It was a sign, perhaps, of its pervasive influence, both for good and for ill, in Irish society, in the last century that people welcomed or bewailed its 'fall' in equal measure. To return for a moment to Giotto I think that at this historic moment – at least in Irish society – the Church as we knew it once, is in fragments. That is not at all to suggest that it is no longer relevant; on the contrary there is an urgent need for those who love the Church – in the best sense of that word – to set about the process of sifting through the broken fragments of the good that remains, and carefully and lovingly restoring, renewing and recreating the Church in Irish society. That the eventual shape of the Church will be different is likely and probably timely but that it is restored and renewed and that it does contribute to society and the world is necessary. The kingdom is bigger than the Church but the Church's role in deepening our awareness of the kingdom through the sacraments and the pastoral life is fundamental.

The society in which we live is also fragmented. As long as poverty and inequality, injustice and violence, abuse and crime exist then the kingdom of God is not fully present. The 'Celtic

Tiger' and a booming economy have only served to highlight the increasing gap that exists between the rich and the poor. The unstable peace that exists in Northern Ireland in the aftermath of the Good Friday Agreement has served to highlight the amount of organised paramilitary crime that still exists and the hold that paramilitary organisations have on local communities. The absence of war is not the same as the presence of peace; just because neighbours don't shoot each other does not mean that they don't hate each other. The cancer of bigotry and sectarianism still exist and a huge amount of work remains to be done to heal old wounds and bring two communities closer together. In recent years there has also been huge prejudice and discrimination against ethnic minorities living in Northern Ireland and against the gay and lesbian community.

So the fragments of Giotto's frescoes are reflected too in a society that is becoming increasingly wealthy but increasingly intolerant of those who are different because of social class, religious background, ethnicity or sexual orientation. There are organisations working hard to bring these fragments together and to restore some dignity to those on the margins of society. Many people working in quiet and unassuming ways are building up God's kingdom among those who are marginalised and oppressed. There is much more that could be done, however, and I imagine that the work of restoration will be a long one.

The experience of living in-between the kingdom present and still in the future, between fragments and their restoration requires that we find something to make sense of all that threatens to assail us and pull us under. We need to see in the fragments another possibility, to believe that they are the echoes of something that once was beautiful, something that can lead us back to God, to the kingdom fully present and fully alive. It is the 'sacred' found in the sacraments of the Church and in the 'sacrament' of family and other relationships that acts as the thread pulling us closer into the final pattern of the kingdom of God. By deepening our understanding of the sacred we bind ourselves together more closely in an intimate relationship with each other and with God our creator. In the sacraments of baptism, confirmation and Eucharist we are bound into the family of the Church where we live out our lives in faith, always conscious of the need for God's mercy in the sacrament of reconciliation. In the sacrament of relationships and in our attention to the created world around us we find other echoes of the sacred, other moments where the kingdom becomes present in our day to day lives. We find the sacred in a person who loves us or needs our love, in a sunset or a painting that draws us out of our inner world of preoccupation, in a poem or a story that surprises us and allows us to understand that we are not alone on the journey we call life. A deepening awareness of the sacred, by attention to the world around us and to prayer, allows us to see all created life in a new way, as sacred in itself, reflecting the Divinity of its maker. We see in another person a reflection of the Divine, worthy of infinite love and dignity. From the unborn child to the dying patient we recognise a soul on its own immortal path to God.

The closer we come to the sacred and the deeper we experience it, the more we become aware of our own inadequacies, our own sinfulness. We recognise the need to turn back, to say that we are sorry and accept the unconditional love of God our Father. We discover that as members of the Church, members of the Body of Christ, and members of society we too are fragmented and broken and in need of loving restoration. We live on the threshold between the kingdom present and still in the future. We live between grace and failure, sin and redemption, between creation, fall and restoration. We await the full realisation of the kingdom in faith, hope and love.

THINGS FALL APART

Things fall apart; the centre cannot hold;
Mere anarchy is loosed upon the world,
The blood-dimmed tide is loosed, and
  everywhere
The ceremony of innocence is drowned...

W.B. Yeats, 'The Second Coming'

'Giotto, Giotto...'

The Thirty-Third Sunday in Ordinary Time, Year C

On 26 September 1997 two earthquakes devastated parts of central Italy. The epicentre of the earthquake was in the Apennine hills and it caused greatest damage in Assisi and several other towns close by. The cathedrals of Orvieto, Urbino, Bevagna and Fabriano were damaged in the earthquake, suffering cracks and fractures in their stonework. The worst damage, however, was sustained in Assisi. At the Basilica of Saint Francis the vaulted ceiling collapsed when the walls buckled and the 700-year-old frescoes fell from their great height crushing four people. Along with two Franciscan friars who were killed an art restorer was crushed beneath the very stones he loved. The woman in charge of the restoration, stood a few days later inside the basilica in tears, lifting scraps of plaster and repeating with reflective sadness: 'Giotto, Giotto...'

I had been to Italy for the first time a year before the earthquake. I had visited Assisi and remember the uphill walk to the wonderful basilica. I remember the feeling of awe when I looked up inside the church at the marvelous cycle of frescoes by Giotto. Here was something permanent, I thought, something eternal in its beauty, something beyond the vicissitudes of time. I felt assured by the beauty of the frescoes, reassured by their age. Here were paintings that moved me, that spoke to me about faith, simplicity, love and trust; in this sense they were personal, assuring my own faith. In another sense, however, they were beyond me in time, part of a bigger picture, something that had been before me and would last beyond me. Their age reassured me of something greater than myself, of a mystery of which I was only a part, of a kingdom beyond the limits of this world, beyond my own.

I was shocked when I learned late in September 1997 that the frescoes had fallen from the ceiling of the basilica as a result of the earthquake. I thought of the devastation that the people of Assisi must have felt. I thought of the families who had lost loved ones in the tragedy, of the Franciscan friars who lost two of their community, and of those who loved Giotto whose work had returned to dust. I thought of those frescoes, of how they had assured and reassured me not so long before. I thought of it as a kind of apocalypse, some terrible ending, of a world bereft of permanence. What was art for if it didn't last, if it was mortal too? The earthquake in Assisi seemed to point up an obvious yet somehow forgotten fact. We feel that great art somehow lays a claim to immortality – that the pyramids will always stand in the burning desert; that the Mona Lisa will smile enigmatically forever, and that the Parthenon will always stand guard over Athens. And yet when art as old and as taken for granted as the frescoes in Assisi returns to bricks and mortar it reminds us of our mortality too. Art, in imitation of life, is also mortal:

When some were talking about the Temple, remarking how it was adorned with fine stonework and votive offerings, he said, 'All these things you are staring at now – the time will come when not a single stone will be left on another: everything will be destroyed'…Then he said to them, 'Nation will fight against nation, and kingdom against kingdom. There will be great earthquakes and plagues and famines here and there; there will be fearful sights and great signs from heaven' (Lk 21:5-6, 10-11).

I thought of Christ's prophecy when I learned about the tragedy in Assisi. I thought of the fear it must have instilled in those who took his words literally. The Temple was at the heart of the Jewish faith, something permanent, the most sacred place. Christ's prophecy was bold for those who could not see that he was talking about his own death. But even as Christ prophesises the end of this world he hints at the creation of a new world when we will win our lives again by endurance:

> You will be betrayed even by parents and brothers, relations and friends; and some of you will be put to death. You will be hated by all men on account of my name, but not a hair of your head will be lost. Your endurance will win you your lives (Lk 21:16-19).

On 26 September 2002, exactly five years after the earthquake that devastated so much of Assisi, a series of restored ceiling and wall frescoes were unveiled in the Basilica of Saint Francis. Five years of patient endurance had restored the fragments to their former glory. It is our belief that Christ will restore the fragments of our lives in glory at the Resurrection.

'THE CEREMONY OF INNOCENCE IS DROWNED...'

The Fifth Sunday of Lent, Year B

A few years ago I drove to a rural parish to hear the first confessions of boys from the local primary school. On the way I was slowed up in traffic and for the few minutes that I sat there I watched a group of about twenty young lambs playing on the slope of a nearby field. And I felt a surge of happiness at this beautiful ceremony of innocence being played out as the sun was setting over the nearby river. And I thought of it again as I watched about sixty small boys of eight make their way to confession for the first time, their uniforms immaculate, and their souls too, except for small sins that they confessed with such innocence and honesty. Probably never again in their lives, I thought, will they make a confession as innocent as this. Because for all their little sins the ceremony of first confession is itself a great ceremony of innocence and it seemed to me as if the playfulness of those young children and those young lambs were one and the same. And it seemed too, no accident that Christ should have presented himself as the Lamb of God.

When I left the parish to make my way home the sun had set and the only reflections on the river now were the distant lights of home. And as the darkness closed in, the lights in a distant city reminded me of another image set in my mind from that time – the lights of Baghdad and the blitzing of that city by coalition bombs in March 2003. The live coverage of the war in Iraq by the media seemed to bring a city and its people, thousands of miles away, right onto our very doorsteps. I thought of children, the same age as those in the small parish in County Tyrone with the same innocence, being drowned in suffering. And I thought of a third ceremony of innocence, this time in Yeats' 'The Second Coming', where he prophesised, in a time of Civil War in Ireland, a terrible culture of violence:

> Things fall apart; the centre cannot hold;
> Mere anarchy is loosed upon the world,
> The blood-dimmed tide is loosed, and everywhere
> The ceremony of innocence is drowned...[1]

There is a fourth ceremony of innocence in a story from the Gospel of John. Christ, the innocent lamb, faces his impending suffering and death. Even John, who fails to mention Christ's agony in the garden because he wants to show Jesus in full control of the situation, is forced to have Jesus say that he is afraid:

> Anyone who loves his life loses it;
> Anyone who hates his life in this world
> Will keep it for the eternal life.
> If a man serves me, he must follow me,
> Wherever I am, my servant will be there too. If anyone serves me, my Father will honour him.
> Now my soul is troubled.
> What shall I say:
> Father, save me from this hour?
> But it was for this very reason that I have come to this hour.
> Father, glorify your name! (Jn 12:25-28)

The other evangelists are probably much more honest when they present Christ as terrified and in great doubt and agony. It is a Christ, I think, that we can relate to more easily. It was as if, when watching live coverage of the war in Iraq, we were living the passion story in our own time. There is something about bombings and shootings that keep the reality of suffering from our eyes, but a close study of the faces of children fleeing Baghdad in the back of trucks gave us, if only for a minute, a sense of terror, an image of suffering and a glimpse of hell. There is a temptation to despair when anarchy is unleashed upon the world; even Christ knew that. But there is another reality, another world that gives us hope. Suffering and violence, even on a global scale, do not have and cannot have the last word. It would do all of us good to reflect on the thoughts of St Augustine who lived through the collapse of the Roman Empire sixteen hundred years ago. Augustine reminded us in his book *City of God* that we have on earth no lasting city. We are called as followers of Christ to build up God's kingdom on earth, a kingdom of truth, love, justice and peace. The search for the kingdom will bring us great suffering, it will call us to challenge all injustice, to free those who are oppressed. We must be obedient to the will of Christ as Christ was to his Father's. St Paul tells us that Christ becomes, for all who obey him, the source of eternal salvation. Christ's victory and his revolution were founded on selfless love. His victory is our victory too. It is the victory of all who suffer and, first and foremost, it is the victory of children who suffer. Unless you become like little children, you will not enter the Kingdom of Heaven. Every act of love, every time we stand against violence and speak up for those with no voice, we restore something of the ceremony of innocence.

Aware Of An Emptiness

The Ascension of the Lord, Year C

Over the last few years as the revelations of cases of clerical child sexual abuse emerged I found myself searching for something permanent in my priesthood to cling to. I became preoccupied for a time, perhaps in a self-indulgent sense, with the disintegration I sensed around me – disintegration of children's lives, of people's faith, of my own sure sense of who I was or who I wanted to be. I was accused by some of exaggeration in my analysis and focus, of a lack of proportion, of a mindset that was unnecessarily negative and even despairing. For all the reassuring words of many friends, colleagues and parishioners I felt a terrible isolation in my mind and in my vocation. The more I read of the pain inflicted on innocent children the more I doubted the innate goodness of people, the perceived innate goodness of the priesthood. I felt like the bruised reed or wavering flame of Isaiah, as if at any minute I might be crushed by one more sadness.

Eventually I was able to begin to articulate how I felt by reading a short story by William Trevor called 'Justina's Priest'. The story begins with Justina making her confession to Father Clohessy. He is aware of her innocence, her handicap, and that she was intellectually immature for her age. He reflects on the contradiction of this sinless girl making her confession and despite the unnecessary act Father Clohessy is moved by Justina. She reveals in her innocence something that has been lost to Father Clohessy's Church, at least the Church as he knew it. Now that the grandeur of his Church has gone, his vocation within it is described as 'bleak'. He is angry when he preaches because he doesn't know what to say to his parishioners anymore, and stumbling from word to word, he searches for ways to disguise his distress. There is a sense in the midst of all of this that Justina is his salvation, at least that her innocence is. After she leaves the confessional Father Clohessy watches her walk down the church, dip her fingers in the holy water and leave. 'The door of the church closed soundlessly behind her and Father Clohessy was aware of an emptiness, of something taken from him.'[2]

My experience of priesthood in the last number of years resonates with such loss. At times I have felt somewhat threadbare, as if everything I had known and loved was beginning to unravel, that with each revelation of abuse the pattern of my priesthood was fading and that holes were showing where once there had been colour. I recall thinking of how fragile it all was, how vulnerable. As a young boy I had grown up in a Church that was strong, respected and solid. There was a permanence that attached itself to the Church. It was trusted and people needed it; it was necessary. Something of that permanence attracted me as a teenager and I was sure that this is what I wanted to devote my life to. But within three years of my time in Maynooth it seemed as if a thread had come loose and over the next ten years each revelation of abuse seemed to pull at the fabric that had once seemed permanent.

In the context of a feeling of deprivation and isolation I read and stayed with the readings for the feast of the Ascension. I thought of Christ's disciples and how they must have felt when he told them that he was leaving them:

> So you see how it is written that the Christ would suffer and on the third day rise from the dead, and that, in his name, repentance for the forgiveness of sins would be preached to all the nations, beginning from Jerusalem. You are witnesses to this.

'And now I am sending down to you what the Father has promised. Stay in the city then, until you are clothed with the power from on high.' Then he took them out as far as the outskirts of Bethany, and lifting up his hands he blessed them. Now as he blessed them, he withdrew from them and was carried up to heaven (Lk 24:46-52).

Christ's disciples looked for permanence too. At the Transfiguration they wanted to build three tents. Throughout the gospel stories they are in denial of Christ's future suffering. Christ is constantly reminding them that he must suffer so as to rise from the dead. At various times the disciples must have felt that their own world was unraveling, not least when Christ was subjected to such a violent death. These were men who had left everything to follow him and who must have felt at times as if they had made a mistake. But they stayed with Christ even after his death. Before his Ascension, Christ had warned the disciples that it was not for them to know times or dates that the Father had decided by his own authority:

'…but you will receive power when the Holy Spirit comes on you, and then you will be my witnesses not only in Jerusalem but throughout Judaea and Samaria, and indeed to the ends of the earth' (Acts 1:8).

There is much that is fragile about life and there is much that is fragile about the Church, but we might take encouragement from Paul's advice to the Hebrews:

'Let us keep firm in the hope we profess, because the one who made the promise is faithful' (10:23).

'WHILE THE WORLD IS FULL OF TROUBLES...'

The Fifth Sunday of Easter, Year C

The world is a more fragile place after the terrorist attacks of 9/11. Both the assault on America and the retaliation it spawned have shaken all of us to greater or lesser degrees. In America and London people have been told what to do in the event of an attack, what measures to take against the immeasurable. However justified or unjustified the fear is we live out our lives in less certain times, conscious of powers beyond our control, of events much bigger than us but of which we are a part. It strikes me that at a time when a sense of 'traditional' community is breaking down, we are being bound together again not by social responsibility but by fear. The community of looking out for one's neighbour has been replaced by the community of looking over one's shoulder. These are communities of anxiety. We are, of course, easily seduced by fear, adjusting to it naturally as a primal instinct. We carry it from childhood, fear of the dark to an adult fear of loss, the tenuous hold we have on our lives and the lives of those we love. For the most part we choose not to think about it but when a city or a country is under threat we can no longer suppress our vulnerability, our knowledge that at any minute our world might be turned upside down.

That sense of vulnerability, both personal and communal, is beautifully articulated in Ian McEwan's novel *Saturday*.[3] The central character Henry Perowne, a neurosurgeon, wakes in the early hours of 15 February, 2003, the day of huge anti-war demonstrations in London. His sleep is anxious and as he looks out of his bedroom window he sees a plane on fire heading for Heathrow. Instantly he thinks that it is a terrorist attack. Later that day he realises that his fears were unfounded and that the plane, whose engine had caught fire, had landed safely. On his way to a squash match he has a minor car accident and becomes embroiled in a violent dispute with a man called Baxter who, Perowne diagnoses crudely, is suffering from Huntington's Disease (a disorder affecting the muscles and accompanied by a progressive dementia). While Perowne manages to extricate himself from the encounter, he is trailed by Baxter for the rest of the day. Baxter later follows Perowne's wife into their home, threatens her with a knife and insists that their daughter undress in front of him. This chapter, in its fragility and potential for such violence, is almost unbearable to read. But Perowne outwits Baxter, throwing him down a flight of stairs. Later he finds himself being called in to Accident & Emergency to operate on his assailant. What began as a paranoid fear about a terrorist attack ended with a much more intimate, personal encounter with violence.

McEwan's *Saturday* reminded me of that beautiful, tragic poem 'The Stolen Child' by W.B. Yeats where the faeries in the poem weave olden dances:

> ...Mingling hands and mingling glances
> Till the moon has taken flight;
> To and fro we leap
> And chase the frothy bubbles,
> While the world is full of troubles
> And is anxious in its sleep.[4]

That anxiety articulated by Yeats, and later by McEwan, took me back to that most angst-ridden and perplexing book of the New Testament, The Book of Revelation (also known by its Greek name Apocalypse). I think it is fair to say that because it is so different from the rest of the New Testament a lot of us tend to avoid it, as if it somehow intimidates us. It appears to me, however, that the preoccupation of its author with the end of times might parallel our own contemporary preoccupation with the fragile state of our world. It was no surprise that in the run-up to the millennium many people looked to its prophecies in much the same way as people might read tarot cards; they sought to divine in its apocalyptic tone a code or a mechanism by which they might understand the historical moment of which they were a part.

From the early second century The Book of Revelation was ascribed to John the Apostle, thought also to be the author of the fourth gospel. However, a seeming discrepancy between the styles of Greek in the two writings led others to believe that it may have been the work of a recognised prophet in the Church, writing for his contemporaries about the year AD 95.[5] It is important to understand the book in its historical context, that of the persecution of Christians by the emperors Nero and Domitian in the second half of the first century. The author is, understandably, hostile to the Roman Empire and looks forward to the coming of the Kingdom:

> Then I saw a new heaven and a new earth; the first heaven and the first earth had disappeared now, and there was no longer any sea. I saw the holy city, and the New Jerusalem, coming down from God out of heaven, as beautiful as a bride all dressed for her husband. Then I heard a loud voice call from the throne, 'You see this city? Here God lives among men. He will make his home among them; they shall be his people, and he will be

their God; his name is God-with-them. He will wipe
away all tears from their eyes; there will be no more
death, and no more mourning or sadness. The world of
the past has gone.' Then the One sitting on the throne
spoke: 'Now I am making the whole of creation new', he
said. (Rev 21:1-5).

The promise of a 'new creation' where God would be present
with his people and would wipe away their tears must have
given Christians, living in first century imperial Rome, the hope
and reassurance they were so desperate for. I suggest that The
Book of Revelation, properly understood, might also provide
for us the reassurance of God's presence in our own world of
empires in which we are assailed by uncertainty and fear.

GRACE OR GRAVITY?

The Eleventh Sunday in Ordinary Time, Year A

In April 2002 Fr Desmond O'Donnell argued in *The Irish Times* that the Church is in good shape compared to the old days. He recognised the immense damage caused by child sexual abuse, the continuing drop in Mass attendance and the falling number of vocations to the priesthood. He went on to ask the question, 'Is this grace or gravity? Is it gravity pulling the Church downwards or is it grace inviting it upwards?' His answer was that it was a moment of grace. I am inclined to agree with him. It was in the good old days, he argues, that the crimes of child abuse were being perpetrated. If, as a result of coming to terms with and coming to the truth of clerical child abuse, the Church becomes more open and ultimately more credible then perhaps, as Fr O'Donnell suggests, the good days of the Church are just emerging.

Part of what were called the good old days was a high level of vocations to the priesthood and the religious life. As well as the many men who devoted their priestly lives to the missions many left Ireland to work in other dioceses because Ireland had too many priests. That is clearly not the case today. I think that the present shortage of priests has been unduly lamented and that at times some of us as priests have indulged in scare-mongering. Of course vocations to the priesthood are fundamental to the life of the Church, but so also are the many gifts and qualities of the laity that we have not yet fully embraced or even endorsed. I feel, for example, that we have become overly protective of the liturgy and have hewn from the work of the people our own priestly altars. In the Book of Exodus, God consecrates a nation to the priesthood:

> You yourselves have seen what I did with the Egyptians, how I carried you on eagle's wings and brought you to myself. From this you know that now, if you obey my voice and hold fast to my covenant, you of all the nations shall be my very own, for all the earth is mine. I will count you a kingdom of priests, a consecrated nation (Ex 19: 4-5).

We have not yet fully explored, I feel, the priesthood of all who are baptised. We need to see the grace of God working in other ways outside the important formalised liturgies of the church. Many people, particularly young people, are actively involved in work relating to justice and care for the environment. Young people are, perhaps, the great untapped resource. Their work in caring for the disadvantaged and the world around them is fundamental to the building up of God's kingdom on earth, a kingdom of truth, love, justice and peace. If their experience and generosity could be more imaginatively embraced in our liturgies and in the formal rituals of our church then we might begin to see a revival where different forms of worship might be accommodated.

It has been a mistake to equate a crisis in terms of numbers for the priesthood with a crisis in the Church. There are many other crises more pressing than falling numbers of vocations. Failing to be creative, imaginative and constructive are failings of a much more serious nature. We need to read the signs of the times, to divine other sources of ministry that will sustain our faithful communities. We have tended, particularly in Ireland, to concentrate our sources and resources on the ordained ministry. As a result we have become myopic in our understanding of ministry to the extent that we have equated ministry with that of ordination. Christ continues to send out disciples, as he did in the gospels, who can proclaim, as the first disciples did, that the kingdom of heaven is close at hand:

> And as you go, proclaim that that the kingdom of heaven is close at hand. Cure the sick, raise the dead, cleanse the lepers, cast out devils. You received without charge, give without charge (Mt 10:7-8).

Never before have there been as many young lay men and women studying theology. Are they not disciples of Christ? Many young men and women have taken study leave for a year to offer their services in countries where there is poverty and social deprivation. I think of a young colleague of mine who spent her summer holidays working with street children in Latin America. Many young people through organisations such as Amnesty International meet to fight against human rights violations. I recall particular students of mine writing off to government officials in order to free a Tibetan nun. I recall their sense of joy when they received news many months later that the nun had been freed unharmed. Are they not disciples of Jesus Christ?

Paul, in his Letter to the Romans, talks about being filled 'with joyful trust in God, through our Lord Jesus Christ' (5:11). It is a beautiful sentiment of trust and one which we might reflect upon as we journey together as a church in this new decade and century. Perhaps the greatest vocation for all of us in these changing and formative times is to lead where there is no road but to leave a path in our tracks.

THE PITY OF IT ALL

Sleep and, asleep, forget
The watchers on the wall
Awake all night who know
The pity of it all

Louis McNeice, 'Cradle Song for Eleanor'

One Week In August

The First Sunday of Lent, Year B

I first met Denise in the last few minutes of her life on a roadside in County Donegal. She was lying on a grass verge at the side of the road where a wheel, which had come loose from a lorry, had thrown her. I came upon the accident a few minutes after it had happened, on my way to holiday in Donegal. I knelt down beside a young teenage girl, just fifteen, as she lay dying. I will never forget it. Having just celebrated the first anniversary of my ordination to the priesthood, I felt as inadequate as I had been eight years earlier when I entered the seminary. In fact I felt even more inadequate since now, at this moment, so much was expected of me. I wanted to be strong for her, not to frighten her, to console her as she left this world. I tried to speak to her in words that would make sense, to anoint her in a way that would heal her fear and lessen her pain. I told her that she would be okay, that God loved her and would look after her. I felt a pain in my throat as sore as I have ever felt, as if at any moment the grief would slice through it and drown me.

Yards from where Denise lay was her younger brother Brian who suffered very severe head injuries. On the other side of the road lay her younger sister Stacey who was also hurt, although not seriously. When Denise died, I kissed her on the forehead and went and prayed with the other two children and their parents. The scale of the suffering for that family was beyond me at that moment; I suspect that it was somewhat beyond them too. There was no time for reflection on what all this meant, everything was immediate, even the grief. It would be hours and days before the full impact of what had happened on that summer's day sank in; until then everyone had to pick up the pieces of a moment that shattered a family forever.

After the children and their parents had been taken off in three ambulances I got back into my car and drove, to where I now had no idea. When someone asked me later in the day where the accident had happened I couldn't tell them. It was 10 August, a beautiful summer's day, not a cloud in the sky. It reminded me of childhood summer days when my parents took us for walks to the park. I started to cry those heavy tears that sit on the surface of your eyes like the oil of sadness. The blue sky sat ahead as if on water. Then suddenly the sky was broken up by a flock of geese flying in a perfect V-shaped formation. It came as a kind of surprise or gift, an epiphany. The goose at the head of the flock empowers and leads the others forward. If for any reason a goose must fall out of the formation because it is injured or sick then two other geese fall out with it and accompany it until it can rejoin. When the goose at the front gets tired it falls back and another moves forward to take its place. It is one of the most beautiful natural displays of mutual care and support, of natural order and reciprocity. But it was tainted by what had just happened, spoiled by human suffering. I felt guilty about the sudden sense of joy I experienced as I watched the geese, as if they mocked the sadness and cursed the darkness. I thought of the remark of the poet Louis McNeice who talked about how, on Good Friday, he would walk up and down the garden, keeping his face austere, trying not to be pleased by the daffodils.[6]

It was only later through reflection and prayer that I was able to come to terms with the awful contradictions of that day. Tragedy and beauty are the contradictions not only of a day but of a lifetime in which we believe that the kingdom of God breaks into a fragmented world and a fragile faith. We experience the kingdom of God as a threshold, present and future, here and beyond us still. That tension or displacement makes us eager for certainties and the assurances of faith. The drama of tragedy and grace lived out in those thirty minutes between a roadside accident and a formation of geese is microcosmic of our lives. We live in the in-between of life, between tragic loss and the vibrancy of life, between chaos and order, despair and hope. We live between God's revelation and his hiddenness.

> After John had been arrested, Jesus went into Galilee. There he proclaimed the Good News from God. 'The time has come', he said 'and the kingdom of God is close at hand. Repent, and believe the Good News' (Mk 1:14-15).

The kingdom is close at hand. I remember as a child waiting for Christmas Day and how the closer it got the further away it seemed. There is something about the presence of the kingdom, the formation of geese, that makes its apparent absence in the tragic death of a young girl so real.

The dictionary defines 'threshold' as 'a strip of wood or stone forming the bottom of a doorway and crossed in entering a house or room'. A threshold, then, by definition is not a destination but a crossing over; it is not a place of arrival or departure but the journey in-between. We journey between the kingdom that is among us and the kingdom that is not yet. It is faith and prayer that enables us to straddle these two worlds between hope and despair, life and death, tragedy and grace.

On 15 August in the same week that Denise had been killed accidentally, twenty-nine people (one pregnant with twins) were deliberately murdered in Omagh, when a bomb planted by the 'Real IRA' ripped through Market Street in the town-centre. It was the feast of the Assumtion of the Blessed Virgin Mary. The litany of death was extraordinarily and tragically comprehensive. The final death toll included unborn twins and grandparents, teenagers anxiously awaiting exam results, young children, fathers and mothers, Catholics and Protestants, visitors and locals. Life in all its vibrancy, creativity and generosity was shamefully wasted – two teenage schoolgirls, working voluntarily in a charity shop, were killed in the explosion which happened just after three o'clock. It was shortly after four o'clock when the horror began to unfold on the television. I watched it in disbelief, still deeply upset about Denise's death only five days earlier. How could people have planned this? What ideology or 'cause' could ever justify such horror? What kind of people could watch the carnage that they had been responsible for unfold? I was due to celebrate the vigil mass that evening. For the first time in my priesthood I felt numb as I celebrated mass. During the homily I juxtaposed the accidental death of a young teenage girl with the deaths and suffering inflicted on innocent people just hours previously. The contrast could not have been more stark. This was different, people had planned it, had known about it for weeks, even months. I felt sick in my stomach, annoyed at how my anger consumed me, hurt by a grief from which, in reality, I was so distant. I wondered about everything that I thought was certain – the goodness of people, the goodness of God, the tenuousness of faith and the distance of the kingdom at that moment.

For all the distance of the kingdom after Omagh, it was the words of St Peter that gave me some consolation for the innocent people who lost their lives that day:

> Why Christ himself, innocent though he was, had died once for sins, died for the guilty, to lead us to God. In the body he was put to death, in the spirit he was raised to life... (1Pet 3:18).

I will never forget that one week in August when the kingdom of God seemed, at the same time, both so remote and so present. I prayed that Denise, who had lost her life in such tragic circumstances, and all the victims of Omagh who had been put to death in such a violent way, would be raised, in the spirit, to life. I prayed the words of the 'Our Father' at mass, 'Thy kingdom come...'

'PLACES WHERE THE SPIRIT DIES...'

The Twenty-Eighth Sunday in Ordinary Time, Year B

I visited Los Angeles once to work for a summer in a parish there. The highlight of my stay was a visit to The Museum of Tolerance. Opened in 1993, to date it has been visited by three and a half million visitors from around the world. It is a high-tech, hands-on interactive museum that focuses on two central themes: the dynamics of racism and prejudice in America and the history of the Holocaust, presented as the ultimate example of man's inhumanity to man. The genesis of the museum, the first of its kind in the world, came from the leadership of the Simon Wiesenthal Centre, the internationally recognised Jewish human rights organisation named in honour of Simon Wiesenthal. Wiesenthal was lucky enough to survive the Nazi death camps of World War II. He did not return to his pre-War profession as an architect, but instead became the conscience and voice for both the Holocaust's six million Jewish victims and the millions of others murdered by the Nazis. His centre, founded in 1977, carries on the continuing fight against bigotry and anti-Semitism and pursues an active agenda in relation to related contemporary issues. The Museum of Tolerance, the educational arm of the Simon Wiesenthal Centre, was founded to challenge visitors to confront bigotry and racism, and to understand the Holocaust both historically and in a contemporary way.

In one part of the museum is the 'Tolerancentre', a room where visitors are asked to confront their own religious, political, cultural and social prejudices. It explores, in a very open and honest way, the history of Civil Rights in America and the role played, in particular, by Martin Luther King. Alongside this exhibition, visitors have access to 'hate sites' on the internet from around the world where people – because of their skin colour, race, sexual orientation, or religious beliefs – are portrayed and defined as little more than vermin. I found myself hugely disturbed by what I saw and read in that room. Every instinct that I had had, every value that I had cherished, was undermined by the intolerance and hatred displayed there. I felt a connection with my own experience of growing up in Northern Ireland, a connection that confirmed my sense of vulnerability, of insecurity in the face of naked hatred and destructive propaganda. I was suddenly aware of the universal nature of bigotry, of the relation between my own particular experience growing up as a young boy in Derry and the universal experience of people throughout the world. I thought of Tom Paulin's poem 'Desertmartin' where he talks about a small local community, deeply religious but divided at the same time, where he sees a strong Presbyterian grace sour and where the 'Word has withered to a few parched certainties'. 'These are the places', Paulin concludes, 'where the spirit dies'.[7]

Bigotry is not confined to a geographical place or a particular historical, cultural moment but to a mindset, a narrowing of our range of vision. It is about borders in our mind rather than borders in our community, blind spots in our own vision rather than blindness in others, the plank in our own eye, not the splinter in our neighbour's. These are the places where the spirit dies, where all that is life-giving in cultural, political, ethnic and religious diversity becomes life-threatening through ignorance, prejudice, discrimination and fear. Our neighbour becomes a threat instead of a gift, someone to be held at arms length rather than someone to be embraced. The perimeter of our world becomes narrower, our experience more shallow. In an age when electronic communications are opening up the global world to us, increasing prejudice and fear are fastening us into our own local exclusive communities. We communicate easily by electronic mail but not by talking, not by opening up our hearts and minds to others different from ourselves. Our political, cultural and religious identities imprison us rather than free us. My own experience of living and working as a priest in Northern Ireland is that the Word that is there to set us free is often withered to a few parched certainties and the fertile soil of healthy Christian communities becomes the barren desert where the seed has fallen but quickly withers away. The Word needs to become nurtured again in our own lives, in the lives of all the different Christian communities that profess it:

> The word of God is something alive and active: it cuts like any double-edged sword but more finely: it can slip through the place where the soul is divided from the spirit, or joints from the marrow; it can judge the secret emotions and thoughts. No created thing can hide from him; everything is uncovered and open to the eyes of the one to whom we must give an account of ourselves (Heb 4:12-13).

Paul's definition and description of the word is beautifully insightful; the word becomes a presence that can slip through the place where the soul is divided from the spirit. It can judge our secret emotions and thoughts and in the end it is to the Word made flesh that we must give an account of ourselves. It is precisely the Word that inspires us to confront our own prejudice and bigotry, to challenge the bigotry of others and so to see in every human being the wonderful gift that he or she is.

A Shaft Of Light On The Debris Of Life

The Second Sunday after Easter, Year A

In 1880, shortly before his death, the Russian novelist Fyodor Dostoyevsky completed his finest novel, *The Brothers Karamazov*. At one level it is a portrait of nineteenth-century Russia, a time of immense poverty and deprivation. On another level, however, the book deals with questions around faith and the existence of God. The story unfolds through two brothers, Ivan and Alyosha. On the one hand, Ivan is a writer with intense revolutionary ideas who voices great doubts about the existence of God; Alyosha, on the other hand, is a religious novice deeply committed to his faith in God. In one very moving passage Ivan tells the story of a young girl caught up in the trap of poverty who is regularly beaten and raped by her stepfather. In the telling of the story, Ivan becomes angry with Alyosha and tells him that belief in God is not worth one little tear of that tortured girl who cried repeatedly to God for help, but in vain. When he has finished telling Alyosha the story, Ivan breaks down in tears and says to him, 'It is not God that I do not accept, Alyosha, I merely most respectfully return him the ticket.'[8]

Recently I spoke to a woman who had suffered a great deal of hurt in her life. She had lost her husband shortly after they were married and then soon afterwards she was diagnosed with cancer. She pointed to a crucifix hanging on the wall of her sitting room and told me, as she began to cry, how she shouted at Christ to get off that cross and help her. She cried because she hurt, she cried because she was helpless, she cried, she said, because she felt her faith was so weak. I didn't want to speak because I felt to do so would have betrayed her pain; what could I possibly say to a woman who did not need Christ to come down to her because she shared his cross beside him? When I went home I thought of the story of Ivan and the little girl in *The Brothers Karamazov*. I thought of Ivan's acceptance of God but not his world; I thought of his anger and of his tears. I thought of another passage too from the first letter of St Peter:

> Through your faith, God's power will guard you until the salvation which has been prepared is revealed at the end of time. This is a cause of great joy for you, even though you may for a short time have to bear being plagued by all sorts of trials; so that, when Jesus Christ is revealed, your faith will have been tested and proved like gold – only it is more precious than gold, which is corruptible even though it bears testing by fire – and then you will have praise and glory and honour. You did not see him, yet you love him; and still without seeing him, you are already filled with a joy so glorious that it cannot be described, because you believe; and you are sure of the end to which your faith looks forward, that is, the salvation of your souls (1 Pet 1:5-9).

'You did not see him, yet you love him...' We talk about 'blind faith', believing without seeing. Faith is deeply personal and incredibly fragile. It is not weak because we question or even shout at God. If a mother in Belfast or Beslan watches her child die as a result of violence and shouts at God in anger or refuses to accept his world, are we to say that her faith is weak? People do not see Christ when they are blinded by pain, and yet somewhere in the brokenness of their hearts they love him. I have often wondered what deep, personal pain the disciple Thomas went through when he needed to touch the hole in the side of Jesus:

> Thomas, called the Twin, who was one of the Twelve, was not with them when Jesus came. When the disciples said, 'We have seen the Lord,' he answered, 'Unless I can see the holes that the nails made in his hands and can put my finger into the holes they made, and unless I can put my hand into his side, I refuse to believe'(Jn 20:24-25).

Perhaps Thomas was justified in his demand for certainty. We do not know what kind of suffering he knew; we do not know what kind of world he did not accept. To shout at God may be the most powerful prayer of all; to refuse to accept a world of injustice is strength not weakness; and to love God without seeing him is the most courageous act of faith.

The German theologian Karl Rahner wrote that prayer, when it is uttered in despair, may be the prayer of a poor, yet faithful heart:

> Despite weakness, depression and weariness, a small shaft is again and again dug by honest labour, and through that shaft a ray of eternal light falls upon a heart buried by the debris of daily life.[9]

'AM I GOING TO DIE?'

The Fifth Sunday of Lent, Year A

My aunt Meta died of cancer at the age of sixty-seven. It was a devastating blow to her family for she was the hub around which they gathered. She was the eldest in a family of six, her mother having lost three other children as infants. She was a woman of remarkable faith, simple and straightforward, but faithful in the richest sense of that word. She was enormously proud when I went off to Maynooth and my ordination was a day that she waited and prayed for. When my grandmother died, it was as if she instantly replaced her as the centre of the family for my mother and aunts and uncles. It was a role she assumed easily, being a woman of great faith and inner strength. She reared her family during the worst of the Troubles in an estate in Derry that was at the centre of much paramilitary activity and harassment from members of the security forces. My abiding memory of her is that whenever anyone was shot – a member of the IRA or a soldier or policeman – she drove to the place where they died and blessed the ground with holy water. It was a remarkably simple but profound gesture that summed up Meta's faith; here was a wonderful theology of blessing or anointing, a making sacred of some terrible brokenness, shining light into the darkest corners of Derry's Troubles. One particular story, perhaps, best illustrates my point. Meta's son was a taxi driver and one evening masked men arrived at her house to wait for her son to come home so that they could use his car for a 'military operation' (often paramilitaries used someone's car when planning an attack on a soldier or policeman). It was part of Meta's innocence that she felt that she could lecture these masked men while they waited about the wrong that they were doing, and it was part of her strength that they let her. She was deeply disturbed that her son's car might be used in the shooting of someone, in the taking of someone else's life. While they waited for her son to come in from work, Meta prayed the rosary in front of these men and prayed that their mission would be foiled. She told me once that she had complete trust in God and that she believed, on this occasion, that he would not allow anything bad to happen. When her son returned home from work in his taxi the masked men wasted no time and took his keys and fled the house. Meta watched from the window as they had problems starting the car; when they discovered that the clutch had burned out, the operation was abandoned and they ran off.

Meta didn't believe that this was evidence of some remarkable miracle, but accepted it easily as an answer to her prayers. She had asked God to intervene and he had.

Meta had been complaining for a long time about pains in her back before she was finally told it was cancer. Her attitude was very positive but the diagnosis was bad, the cancer was terminal. Meta wouldn't and didn't accept it; she had asked God for help in the past and he had answered her prayers. Besides, her nephew was now a priest and each day that I saw her she thanked me for remembering her at mass because she believed that would cure her. I found it difficult at times visiting her. She was absolute in her faith and I wanted with all my heart to believe that it was possible for the cancer to disappear. I doubted this, not because of the medical certainty, but because my faith wasn't up to it, wasn't a patch on Meta's. I used to leave her bedside with a lump in my throat as I promised her I would remember her in mass the following day. I thought of Mary and Martha who sent word to Jesus that Lazarus was ill:

> There was a man named Lazarus who lived in the village of Bethany with the two sisters, Mary and Martha, and he was ill. It was the same Mary, the sister of the sick man Lazarus, who anointed the Lord with ointment and wiped his feet with her hair. The sisters sent this message to Jesus, 'Lord, the man you love is ill.' On receiving the message, Jesus said, 'This sickness will end not in death but in God's glory, and through it the Son of God will be glorified' (Jn 11:1-4).

When the hospital had done all they could, Meta was sent home to her daughters where her family and different nurses cared for her every day. I used to visit her once a day to bring her communion and she loved that important ritual. She felt that the Holy Communion gave her an inner strength that would make her better. But within weeks, Meta had deteriorated rapidly; deep down she must have known that things were bad. One afternoon, after I had given her Holy Communion, she asked the family to leave the room and for me to stay behind. She then asked me two questions, both of which saddened me in different ways. When I sat beside her and took her hand, she looked me straight in the face and said, 'Gary, am I going to die?' She must have read the sadness in my face because she squeezed my hand as if to make it easy, as if to say 'go on, I can take it'. I told her that she was seriously ill and that there was nothing that the doctors could do but that God would take her when she was ready. I told her that she had nothing to worry about, that she had lived such a life of faith and love that God would welcome her home with open arms. And then she asked me something that saddened me even more: 'Does God love me?' Maybe it came with tremendous insecurity at that moment or maybe, even for this woman of remarkable faith, there was a niggling doubt about God's love for her. I could hardly answer her, but when I did I reminded her of those victims of violence that she had blessed so faithfully over the years and how, in her own simple way, she had lit a candle in her own local community rather than curse the darkness.

When Jesus arrives in Bethany, Lazarus is already dead and in the tomb, but Jesus says to Martha:

> I am the resurrection.
> If anyone believes in me, even though he dies he will live,
> and whoever lives and believes in me
> will never die (Jn 11:25-26).

When Jesus orders Lazarus to come out of the tomb, the dead man walks out and Jesus says, 'Unbind him, let him go free' (Jn 11:44). Meta didn't get better, but in that last moment we shared I knew that Christ loved her and that Meta received a great peace, safe in the knowledge that God would take care of her. I prayed silently to myself, 'Lord, unbind her, let her go free'. And he did.

ACCUMULATING SILENT THINGS WITHIN US

The Fifth Sunday of Lent, Year C

It was only as an adult that I began to realise that I first learnt to accumulate silent things within myself in my childhood. I was a boy of ten or eleven looking at a photograph of the remains of a car blown up by a bomb that a British soldier had attempted to defuse in Belfast. He was killed instantly in the blast. I took the paper to my bedroom so that I could grieve silently because, although I didn't fully understand the hateful politics around me, I knew enough to know that one did not cry publicly for a soldier. I remember the story only vaguely, something to do with a crowded shopping area and the soldier being sent in to defuse a bomb, to defuse a threat to the lives of others. I saw him in my mind as a child might, as a dad possibly, a son, a person putting himself in danger to protect others. I went cold at the thought of those hours, those minutes when he approached the car; what thoughts raced through his mind? What memories? Or perhaps there was nothing, just this, the job to be done quickly and quietly. Then the explosion – would he have had any sense of it, if only for a split second, any chance to regret things, to shrink his face in fear of a moment already happening, a death already over? At the time I cried sorely for him, for his family, for myself in my isolation, my grief, deafened by the silence within me.

I hated growing up during the Troubles when every death was qualified by creed or job; there was revulsion in our own community when a Catholic was killed, a revulsion qualified when someone was shot in retaliation. A soldier or member of the police force was fair game and I was sick at the celebratory way in which their deaths were announced by some. How could the ending of someone's life be cheered on as if the opposing team had just missed a penalty kick? What had happened to our common humanity, our innate sympathy and empathy for another human being's suffering? How could a uniform or a balaclava reduce someone's life to being worthless, so that, as they bled to death, others jumped for joy? Gradually, the silence ate away at me until an anger grew inside me, an anger I have fought for years, an anger that despises the narrowness of political ideologies and the suffocation of tunneled-vision communities. It was not only a source of anger for me, but one of suffering too. It reminds me now of a remark by Gaston Bachelard: 'What is the source of our first suffering? It lies in the fact that we hesitated to speak... It was born in the moment when we accumulated silent things within us.'[10]

As I grew up, I became more sensitive to the deep hurts that had scarred my community. I began to read about the first Civil Rights marches in Derry and the naked discrimination that many people in the Catholic community suffered for years. There was discrimination in housing, in jobs and in education. The really deep hurts came from institutional injustice and in particular I learned about the terrible events of Bloody Sunday and the deep impact those killings had on a community already suffering great injustice. I never fully appreciated the need for an inquiry into those killings by British soldiers until an aunt of mine died twenty-five years after Bloody Sunday. Throughout her life she was friendly with a woman who had lost her husband on that day. He was a good man, shot while trying to console others who were dying. She took me to one side at the wake and said, 'Father, would you say a mass so that my husband's name is cleared?' I will never forget it and I have prayed since for her husband and all those killed on that day. Had I been wrong, then, as a young boy with no knowledge of what had gone on in Derry for years, to have cried for that soldier who died defusing that bomb? Had I betrayed people in my community who knew what suffering really was, who had lost loved ones whose names were further sullied in later inquiries? I began to see that there was no conflict of interests on my part, no mistake as a child. Instead I recognised the universality of suffering: from the soldier's death in a car bomb, to the man shot dead in cold blood by some other soldier. I came to the conclusion that the only betrayal as a Christian is to betray the humanity of another person, soldier or civilian, friend or enemy.

'The Shield of Achilles' by W.H. Auden is probably one of the most poignant poems about the pity of violence and warfare. The last verse of that poem reads:

> That girls are raped, that two boys knife a third,
> Were axioms to him, who'd never heard
> Of any world where promises were kept
> Or one could weep because another wept.[11]

The ability to empathise with another's suffering is what makes us human. To cry because of another's pain, even if we do not know him or her, is at the heart of what it means to be compassionate, from two Latin words meaning to suffer with someone. For me the most beautiful expression of sympathy in scripture is the story of the woman caught in adultery. The scribes and the Pharisees had allowed the cold legalities of the law to freeze their sympathy so that they could stone a woman to death without a second thought:

The scribes and the Pharisees brought a woman along who had been caught committing adultery; and making her stand there in full view of everybody, they said to Jesus, 'Master, this woman was caught in the very act of committing adultery, and Moses has ordered us in the Law to condemn women like this to death by stoning. What have you to say?' They asked him this as a test, looking for something to use against him. But Jesus bent down and started writing on the ground with his finger. As they persisted with their question, he looked up and said, 'If there is one of you who has not sinned, let him be the first to throw a stone at her' (Jn 8: 3-7).

The writing in the sand creates a space for reflection, a space perhaps where the scribes and Pharisees realise, in sympathy, what they are doing. We all need to create that space for sympathy in our own minds so that we can see other possibilities, other worlds where promises are kept and one can weep because another wept.

First Day At School

The Twenty-Fourth Sunday in Ordinary Time, Year C

My only two nephews began school on a Wednesday. Fearghal and Aodhan are four-year-old twins. Parents who have been through that huge day in the life of their children will appreciate the joy and the pain of it. There's something almost microcosmic about it as an experience of our lives as a whole. How often in our lives is our happiness tinged by loss, tinged by its own fragility, tinged by the fragility of others? How fragile must Fearghal and Aodhan have appeared to their mother as she let go of their hands and told them that they would be fine. She worried about Fearghal who was less enthusiastic than Aodhan and was quiet as he put on a uniform he would wear for another seven years. Aodhan was excited, glad to be leaving the house early in the morning for a whole new adventure. What must have crossed their minds as they arrived at the school gates? What kind of sense did they make of it all, if any? Apparently Fearghal stood nervously at the door of the classroom, hesitant, turning round towards his mother. Aodhan ran on in to the classroom embracing the wonder of it all – a new place and new people. The teacher saw Fearghal standing at the door and prompted Aodhan to encourage him. And then in a simple but lovely gesture Aodhan put his arm round his twin, walked him into the room and sat beside him on those tiny chairs the rest of us can only vaguely remember from our own first school days. Deirdre waited along with many other anxious parents to collect them at one o'clock and hear their stories of day one at school. She must have been taken back to that moment of expectancy when her two boys were twinned inside her. Now they would run from their first day at school into her arms and be hugged, foetal once again. She wasn't disappointed for they told her every detail of that milestone in their lives.

On the same Wednesday Chechen rebels took over a school in Beslan, in southern Russia, and held children and teachers at gunpoint. A sudden explosion in the school hall seemed to have prompted the hostage-takers to begin shooting indiscriminately. In the three-day crisis that followed well over three hundred people, many of them children, were killed.

I thought of Aodhan and Fearghal as I watched the broken and naked children run into their mothers' and fathers' arms on that same Wednesday, when children from Derry and children from Beslan shared their first day at school together. And I thought of Deirdre as I watched the pictures of mothers and fathers whose children never ran out to tell them the story of their first day. The images of parents, in tears, watching as the hall in which their children were imprisoned exploded, will stay with me. Especially poignant was the memory of the little girl who climbed out through a window naked and then, disoriented, climbed back in moments before the ceiling collapsed. For days afterwards parents searched hopelessly for their lost children. Where had they gone? Had they burned in the explosion?

It's tempting to lose faith in the world; it's tempting to no longer believe in the goodness of human beings, and it's tempting, in the end, to lose faith in a God who, we are told, is all-powerful and all-loving. I can sympathise with the holocaust survivor and Nobel Laureate, Elie Wiesel who, after experiencing the concentration camps as a child, refused to prostrate himself at the ceremony of Rosh Hashanah, the Jewish New Year. There is no adequate response or sense to be made of such a blackening darkness. When I watched parents searching frantically for their children, I thought of Christ searching for the sheep that was lost:

> What man among you with a hundred sheep, losing one, would not leave the ninety-nine in the wilderness and go after the missing one till he found it? And when he found it, would he not joyfully take it on his shoulders and then, when he got home, call together his friends and neighbours? 'Rejoice with me', he would say, 'I have found my sheep that was lost' (Lk 15:4-6).

Here we see the care and compassion of Christ for the individual, for the one. Of course, in the context of the above reading from Luke's gospel, the lost sheep represents the sinner, not a child separated from its parents. There is a profound sense, however, in which the lost child of Beslan and the lost sinner are brought terribly together. Violence, both global and local, makes us lose our way. There is a separation as great as that between a parent and their child and that is the separation, the estrangement of sin. One of the most powerful manifestations of sin in our world today is the fragmentation of our communities as a result of violence. We are at a crossroads in our world where the temptation to cause violence in a school hall or in our own homes will take us further and further away from our God. There is need for a deep and profound spirit of repentance in our world, our country and our homes.

Raspberry Picking

The Fifteenth Sunday in Ordinary Time, Year C

The first border we ever learned of as children was close to the house we grew up in. We played with boys in our own street but not beyond that, not beyond the field that we shared in our local community. That a border actually existed outside of the hawthorn hedge that divided two fields and the fertile imaginations of young tribal boys is unlikely, but we believed it. What I remember as fact were the raspberry bushes that had overgrown and outgrown a number of old vegetable plots; they had long become redundant but my father could tell me the name of every previous owner. A lovely old neighbour of mine made raspberry jam in the summer and she used to ask my brother and I if we would collect the berries for her. I associate that time with the seemingly endless summer holidays rolling out in front of me, like the field we crossed to pick the fruit, and as sweet as the pot of jam we received in thanks. There was nothing to sully it, nothing to steal the sweetness of those childhood days.

We had made the short journey before, crossing over the border, real and imaginary. One afternoon in July we made the journey again and carried with us a sand bucket we took as children to the beach. The old vegetable plots were empty and the raspberries were ripe for the picking. There were faint noises beyond the field of boys playing, boys we didn't really associate with, boys we had made our enemies in the folklore of that close-knit community. Everything was in abundance, the sunlight, the smells of summer and the glorious tender fruit that bled and bruised crimson if it wasn't handled with care. As we filled the bucket, even the light weight of the berries damaged each other, and those at the bottom bled softly. Our neighbour would be proud of us when we returned with the harvest.

We were so excited by the crop we had taken, and perhaps a little greedy, that the four boys were behind us before we could see them coming. 'Are you Catholics or Protestants?' they asked us, as if we knew. We didn't, but suddenly the border that people talked about was no longer imaginary and we had stepped over it. They must have known what a Catholic was and what a Protestant was, and therefore we should have known, but we didn't, and so we guessed. 'We're Catholics', we said, whatever that meant. In the end it meant a lot. One boy took the bucket of raspberries from us and tipped them out on the grass; then the four boys jumped on them as we ran. We didn't look back until we were safely home and crying. My last memory of that encounter was one boy holding up the bucket and the bitter juice dripping from the sides, as bitter as the memory of that summer's day. My mother sat us down to tell us, finally, what a Catholic was and what a Protestant was; she was hurt at having to tell us, we were hurt at having to know. The summers were never the same again:

> Jesus replied, 'A man was on his way down from Jerusalem to Jericho and fell into the hands of brigands; they took all he had, beat him and then made off, leaving him half dead. Now a priest happened to be travelling down the same road, but when he saw the man, he passed by on the other side. In the same way a Levite who came to the place saw him, and passed by on the other side. But a Samaritan traveller who came upon him

was moved with compassion when he saw him. He went up and bandaged his wounds, pouring oil and wine on them. He then lifted him onto his own mount, carried him to the inn and looked after him' (Lk 10:30-34).

Earlier in Luke's gospel, Jesus sent messengers on ahead of him to Jerusalem. We are told that they went into a Samaritan village to make preparations for him but that the people would not receive him because he was making for Jerusalem. 'Seeing this, the disciples James and John said, "Lord, do you want us to call down fire from heaven to burn them up?" But he turned and rebuked them, and they went off to another village' (Lk 9:54-56).

Jesus lived in a country and in a world of borders. The Jews despised the Samaritans because they had inter-married with foreign invaders and had their own temple outside of Jerusalem. Christ was well aware of the hatred that existed between the two when he told the parable. But this story demonstrates how compassion and pity help us to ignore barriers and to love the individual. I imagine that the Samaritan was a good man who would have helped anyone in need; the fact that the man in need of help was a Jew was irrelevant.

We too live in a country and in a world of borders, some imaginary and others real. The barriers that we construct in our heads are as dangerous, if not more so, than the ones we construct with bricks. We can easily demolish physical barriers; it is much more difficult to demolish barriers of prejudice and hate. The parable of the Good Samaritan suggests that we focus on the person, the human being who cries out for help. The way to demolish barriers of prejudice is to reflect on our common humanity, the tears that we share.

THE BANALITY OF EVIL

The Eighteenth Sunday in Ordinary Time, Year A

I had never heard of Stephen McCann until I came across a record of his death in *Lost Lives*, an index of all those who lost their lives in the Northern Ireland Troubles. Under number 1829 in the book his entry reads 'October 30, 1976. North Belfast. Civilian, Catholic, 21, single, student'. The statements of fact, such as date, place of residence, religious denomination, marital status and age which accompany each entry in *Lost Lives* lend an air of ordinariness to these most extraordinary and sad deaths. Next to the Jerusalem Bible, I consider *Lost Lives* to be the most sacred book I have and when I can find the strength to read it, I do so with profound respect, for here is a tragic epic, the proportions of which are to be found in each life and death recounted in a simple human way.[12]

Stephen McCann was from the Cavehill district of north Belfast and was a founder member of the Witness for Peace movement and the author of the song 'What Price Peace?' which was sung at many peace rallies. On 30 Saturday October 1976 he and his girlfriend had attended a dance at Queen's University students' union. At the same time a group that became known as the Shankhill Butchers had been drinking in a loyalist club and after it closed 'decided to go out and get a Taig'. They spotted Stephen and his girlfriend walking home and closed in on them. One of them pushed

Stephen's girlfriend to the ground while the others bundled Stephen into the car. They drove off and stopped at a house where they collected a gun and a knife. They drove to Glencairn where they shot Stephen in the head and cut his throat with a butcher's knife.

Stephen's death is only one of 3,637 deaths recorded in *Lost Lives,* but it is the focus on the individual human stories behind each death that makes the reality of suffering and evil tangible. What I found most disturbing about the account of Stephen's death, apart from the irony of his conviction about peace and the brutal way in which he met his death, was how his killers after a night's drinking could decide to murder another human being on the way home, in much the same way that someone might decide to stop off for fish and chips when the pubs closed.

In 1963, the political thinker Hannah Arendt published *Eichmann in Jerusalem,* the subtitle of which 'A Report on the Banality of Evil', caused much debate.[13] Her thesis was that the German Nazi, Adolf Eichmann, and other functionaries of totalitarianism, were best understood neither as monsters nor as cogs in the Nazi machine, but rather as 'terribly and terrifyingly normal'. She argued that Eichmann lacked imagination and was simply a banal and ordinary perpetrator of evil. Arendt attempted to expose the ordinariness that enables a human being to blur completely the difference between right and wrong. It struck me in reading *Lost Lives* that while many killings centered around the sectarian politics of Northern Ireland, there was much too that was 'banal' about the circumstances in which so many were murdered. One has only to pick up the daily newspapers to read stories of people bludgeoned to death or raped and strangled to appreciate Arendt's thesis that there is something terribly 'ordinary' or 'banal' about evil. I wondered too, as I watched Mel Gibson's *Passion of the Christ,* how banal Christ's torture and execution were. Were the Roman soldiers, who scourged Christ so violently at the pillar, or who hammered nails into his hands really monsters or were they simply thoughtless men, lacking imagination, for whom the line separating good and evil had become irreversibly blurred? Or the religious leaders who were quite prepared to stone a woman to death for committing adultery; were they innately evil or just ordinary faithful people carried away by the letter of the Law? The story of the beheading of John the Baptist has always struck me as the epitome of the banality of evil. The daughter of Herodias dances for Herod and delights him so much that he promises her anything she wants. Prompted by her mother, she asks for John the Baptist's head on a dish:

> The head was brought in on a dish and given to the girl who took it to her mother. John's disciples came and took the body and buried it; then they went off to tell Jesus. When Jesus received this news he withdrew by boat to a lonely place where they could be by themselves (Mt 14:11-13).

Are we to suppose that Herodias was evil through and through? Are the 'monsters' that we read about in the papers who kill innocent people innately evil, possessed from birth, and damned to hell? At what moment does someone no longer recognise or care about the line between good and evil. Is it possible that such a line divides not the good from the bad but each human heart? What capacity do each of us have for evil and what is it that helps us to hold the line, to tow the line between actions that are moral and those that damage other human beings? It seems to me that the degree to which we hold the line is proportionate to our ability to sympathise with another human being. We do not commit evil, not because we are not capable of it but because we stop ourselves, our sense of another's suffering holds us back. It is our innate ability to connect at a human level with each other that makes us fundamentally moral people. We know what it is to hurt and so we refrain from hurting others. From a Christian perspective we recognise in another human being someone created in the image and likeness of God, a temple of God's Holy Spirit. Evil is often 'banal' because those who commit it are not monsters but are ordinary; they have somehow become disconnected at an emotional level with other human beings so much so that they cannot sympathise with the victim they choose to hurt. The screams of their victims do not resonate with their own inner pain and darkness. Hannah Arendt's judgement about the banality of evil should frighten us because it no longer becomes possible to categorise people simply as 'good' and 'bad'. The line separating it passes through the heart of each of us and reminds us of the need to reflect on the judgements we make in the context of our wider human family, in sympathy and faith.

FINDING THE SACRED

Only in dialogue and interaction with the moral and the artistic, as they flourish today, can the religious hope to renew faith.

Enda McDonagh, *Faith In Fragments*

THE DIVINER AND THE WOMAN AT THE WELL

The Third Sunday of Lent, Year A

In one of his short stories, 'The Diviner' Brian Friel tells the story of Nelly Devenny who decides to remarry after her first husband dies in a road accident. When she marries Arthur Doherty, the squinting village of Drumeen watches his every move because he is a stranger. However, they rally round Nelly, six months later, when they learn the tragic news that Arthur hasn't come home from fishing on the lake. They drive to the lake with Nelly and the parish priest and there they find Arthur's boat, waterlogged and swaying on its keel, in the shallow water along the shore. Two frogmen search the lake in vain after their own amateur search fails. When the frogmen leave, McElwee, one of the locals, suggests they send for a diviner. 'The diviner was McElwee's idea,' Friel writes:

> The postman admitted that he knew little about him except that he lived somewhere in the north of County Mayo, that he was infallible with water, and that his supporters claimed that he could find anything provided he got the smell of the truth in it.[14]

McElwee and the diviner set out onto the lake in a small boat, and from an old newspaper, the diviner unwraps a Y-shaped twig, which he holds in his hands with the tail of the Y pointing away from him. Friel's story ends with the quivering twig and

Arthur Doherty's body being pulled out of twenty feet of water. While the priest says the rosary, the diviner waits for someone to drive him back to County Mayo.

The diviner, in Friel's story, is almost a kind of priest-like figure searching beneath the surface of things for the truth. It's interesting that the parish priest in the story is threatened by the diviner's presence. And the other characters in the story, also, can only see the surface of things. When Arthur Doherty arrives in the village they look at the kind of clothes he wears so that they can tell if he is wealthy or not. The parish priest watches to see if he attends Mass or not. It's all surface stuff and so it's not surprising that when tragedy strikes the community is helpless and cannot cope. Only the diviner with his gift of seeing beyond the surface of things is able to find Arthur Doherty's body and bring the tragedy to an end.

It seems to me that there is a connection to be made between Friel's story and the gospel story of the Samaritan woman at the well:

> On the way he [Jesus] came to the Samaritan town called Sychar, near the land that Jacob gave to his son Joseph. Jacob's well is there and Jesus, tired by the journey, sat straight down by the well...When a Samaritan woman came to draw water, Jesus said to her, 'Give me a drink.'...The Samaritan woman said to him, 'What? You are a Jew and you ask me, a Samaritan, for a drink?' – Jews, in fact, do not associate with Samaritans (Jn 4: 5-10).

Arthur Doherty was made to feel a stranger in the village of Drumeen. The woman at the well would have been made to feel a stranger as a Samaritan, outside of her own Samaritan ghetto. In Friel's story Nelly was bereaved twice. The woman at the well had lost five husbands. And almost instantly, like the diviner in Friel's story, Christ could see beyond the surface of this woman's life. He could see an inner sadness and pain. It was as if he knew this woman intimately. He knew her thirst:

> Whoever drinks this water
> will get thirsty again;
> but anyone who drinks the water that I shall give
> will never be thirsty again:
> the water that I shall give
> will turn into a spring inside him, welling up to eternal
> life (Jn 4: 13-14).

When the woman hurries back to tell the town's people what has happened, she utters those beautiful words, 'Come and see a man who has told me everything I ever did; I wonder if he is the Christ?' (Jn.4: 29). Christ sees beyond the shallow waters of this woman's life to the hidden depths of hurt and sadness. The woman draws water from the well but Christ offers her something more. 'The water that I shall give will turn into a spring inside [you], welling up to eternal life' (Jn.4: 14). The living water that Christ offers is the water of God's infinite love for this woman, a love that can steal away her deepest pain and sadness. It is one of the most beautiful stories told in the New Testament.

The great danger for all of us in life is to live on the surface of things. We are afraid to go inwards because there we are at our most vulnerable. There we must face our fears and our broken relationships. But there too is the source of all our kindness, all our hope and all our love. And so it is only by going inwards and facing our own failures and inadequacies that we learn the truth of things and that we can learn to love again. The truth for us as Christians is that we are in constant need of the divine and divining gift of God's grace. Through that grace God will lead us to the very source of inner peace, an acceptance, in love, of our own fragile selves and our fragile neighbours.

THE MAGICIAN'S CAP

The Third Sunday of Easter, Year C

I have never had any real interest in fishing except that as a
youngster my father would take my brother Keith and myself
with him to the river Faughan on a Saturday. Keith would fish
and I would watch and if the weather was bad I would sit,
counting down the hours and the minutes until we got home
to a warm fire and a warm dinner. Occasionally, my father
would fish at a place called Ardmore where the salmon tried,
mostly in vain, to jump the carry and make their way up the
river. I could easily pass a day like that where I would count
how many made it up stream and how many didn't. And
then, like counting sheep, I would get tired and we would go
home.

When the salmon didn't 'show', as the fishermen called it,
I was always disappointed. Then one day my father
introduced me to an old man nicknamed 'Macca'. He knew
exactly where the salmon lay, my father told me, and could
make them appear just by taking off his cap and blocking out
the sun. At the age of seven this seemed like some kind of
magic to me. And so Macca and myself walked the riverbank
and then we stopped. He pointed to water underneath a large
tree and he told me that we would see a salmon there. The
whole ritual was fascinating. The old man prostrated himself
on the slope of the riverbank and carefully took off his cap.
Then he told me to look carefully into the brown water. 'Can

you see it?' he asked me; 'Can you see the salmon?' I could see nothing in the bright sun except the faint shadows of a small boy and an old man. And then he said to me, 'look in the shadow of the cap... can you see it now?' And then, like some miracle of the fishes, suddenly I saw a silver fish motionless except for its fin which swung like the pendulum of a clock. When I went home that night I couldn't get this old magician, who could make salmon appear in the shadow of his cap, out of my head.

> Later on Jesus showed himself again to the disciples. It was by the Sea of Tiberias, and it happened like this: Simon Peter, Thomas called the Twin, Nathanael from Cana in Galilee, the sons of Zebedee and two more of his disciples were together. Simon Peter said, 'I'm going fishing.' They replied, 'We'll come with you.' They went out and got into the boat but caught nothing that night. It was light by now and there stood Jesus on the shore, though the disciples did not realise that it was Jesus. Jesus called out, 'Have you caught anything, friends?' And when they answered, 'No', he said, 'Throw the net out to starboard and you'll find something'. So they dropped the net, and there were so many fish that they could not haul it in (Jn 21:1-6).

I've often wondered if this story, recorded by John, is a miracle story. The disciples on the sea of Tiberias catch nothing all night we are told. And then Jesus asks them to throw out their nets again and we are told that they caught so many fish that they could not haul the nets in. I'm tempted to think that the fish were there all the time but that the disciples couldn't see them. Perhaps the story is not so much a miracle story as a story about sight and seeing things. Not only did the disciples not see the fish but they also failed to recognise Jesus until Peter called out 'It is the Lord'. I'm convinced that if there is a miracle in today's story, then it's a miracle of vision, patience and faith.

All of us in our day to day lives meet Christ in some shape or form. We might meet him in the friend who has just been diagnosed with cancer or in the son struggling with drug addiction. We might meet him in the young mother who has just lost a child or in the young father who has just lost his spouse. We might meet him in the husband or wife whose partner has just walked out on them or in someone suffering from depression. Or we just might meet Christ in those we love and who we take for granted. All of us will meet him today but we might not recognise him.

There is a way of seeing things that we call faith. We need to be open to the Christ in other people. We need to be open to the Christ in ourselves. God will not appear in the spectacular but in the ordinary. In the Old Testament, God was found in the breeze and the gentle quiet. Christ saw the fish in the story from John's gospel. Macca saw the salmon in a quiet river pool in the shade of a cap. He taught me, at the age of seven, a way of seeing things.

THE DYING FIRE

The Second Sunday of Lent, Year C

I grew up in two houses on the same street in Derry. I was the oldest in the family and when I was eight my grandmother asked me if I would stay with her at night because she lived on her own. We lived in number three and my grandmother lived in number six so that my two homes faced each other. I thought it was great because for the first time in my life I had a room of my own with a huge double bed. My grandfather, who died two years before I was born, had a great collection of books, which I loved to read although I couldn't understand most of them. But what sticks out in my mind most from that time of my life was an open fire that I had in my bedroom and a haunting image of the crucifixion that hung opposite my bed. My grandmother had no central heating and during the winter in the severe frost she lit a fire in my bedroom to ensure that the water pipes didn't freeze over. She used to sit beside it and poke the dying embers until I slept. When she turned the light out in the room I used to watch the glow of the fire on her face. She never read but just sat transfixed and transfigured by the glow. Now that I look back as an adult I wonder what she was thinking of at that time and what the glow reminded her off. Did she remember sitting round the fire with my grandfather before he died? My grandfather was a pipe smoker and I wondered did she miss the sweetness of his pipe tobacco and the sweetness of his life? Did she miss her children who'd all grown up now and had children of their own? Did she feel a sense of loss as she watched the fire gradually dying out? Years later when I studied Latin in school it came as no surprise to discover that the Latin word 'focus' meant a hearth.

I remember that time as one of the most secure in my life. I remember even then, as a young boy, knowing that this was special and that this was what happy meant. If I could have suspended that moment outside of time and stayed there, I would have. As I look back to that moment now I realise that perhaps my grandmother was reflecting on loss in her own life, a loss mirrored in the dying fire which threw its light across her transfigured face. Perhaps the glow that flickered across the painting of the crucifixion was another reminder too of the personal loss and suffering that she had suffered in her own life. Now that I reflect again on that moment I see that it prefigured loss in my own life.

I lived with my grandmother for most of the next ten years; she died on 24 August 1989, a week before I went off to Maynooth. It was the first time I felt real loss in my own life; I was eighteen. The painting of the crucifixion stills hangs opposite my bed in my bedroom.

> he [Jesus] took with him Peter and John and James and went up the mountain to pray. As he prayed, the aspect of his face was changed and his clothing became brilliant as lightning... Peter said to Jesus, 'Master, it is wonderful for us to be here; so let us make three tents, one for you, one for Moses and one for Elijah.' – He did not know what he was saying. As he spoke, a cloud came and covered them with shadow; and when they went into the cloud the disciples were afraid (Lk 9:28-29, 33-34.)

The story of the Transfiguration brings the two realities of our lives – joy and suffering – together. Peter, James and John are overwhelmed with joy at the transfigured face of Christ. And they are so overwhelmed that they want to make the moment permanent by building three tents. It's one of the most beautiful human stories in the New Testament. Peter, one of the closest disciples of Christ, wants the moment to last. In the intense joy of the moment he has forgotten that Christ must suffer and he's reminded very dramatically when a cloud comes and covers them with shadow. The transfigured face of Christ is just a glimpse of the glory of Christ in his resurrection.

I believe that in life we are given great moments of joy as glimpses of our eternal happiness with God. A young mother asked me once what I thought heaven was like. She has a beautiful nine-year-old daughter. I told her to imagine the happiest moment she could with her daughter when, for a moment, she didn't worry about her growing up or the harm that might come to her in life – that's what heaven is like but the moment lasts forever and there's no fear of loss. Until then we must live our lives between joy and sadness, happiness and loss, Good Friday and Easter Sunday.

God Our Mother

The Fourth Sunday of Lent, Year B

Just weeks before my ordination my only niece was born. There was, of course, great excitement in our home. She was my parents' first grandchild, my first niece or nephew and most especially my brother's and his wife's first child. They called her Caoimhe. I was honoured to be asked to be her godfather. I constantly marveled at the gift that she was, how a tiny child could evoke such love and generate such happiness. I decided that at my first mass I would like her to be brought forward at the offertory procession as a gift. I felt that she was another presence, another real presence who was 'God's work of art', someone who, in her innocence and vulnerability, had the ability to save us, to draw us away from our selfishness towards a love that was sincere and pure. Our love for her became a symbol, a love that is the source of our first being, our own birth, the creative and redemptive love of God our Father.

As she got older and began to crawl I was astonished at how quickly she learned, soaking up everything around her. I recall visiting her one day and watching her as she was lost in her own little world playing with toys on the floor. Her mother, Deirdre, tip-toed slowly up behind her and then, in an instant, scooped her up and hugged her and kissed her. I remember the burst of joy across Caoimhe's face, the way her whole body turned in towards her mother and embraced her. This was a surprise moment, something unexpected, when Deirdre felt the need to shower her first-born with her love. Caoimhe was unaware of it almost until it was over, but how that moment and that spontaneous expression of love must have burned inside her afterwards.

It struck me afterwards that that simple gesture might come close to what we mean by 'grace'. Grace is a freely given gift, a spontaneous act of love, a surprise moment when God scoops us up in his love and that love remains within us afterwards as an afterglow of faith and acceptance. It also struck me that we must have the disposition of a child if we are to accept that love unconditionally, if we are to turn towards God instinctively and embrace Him. Perhaps when Christ told us that we would not enter the kingdom of God unless we became like little children he meant precisely that, unless we understood that we are completely dependent on God as a parent. At that moment, Caoimhe had no sense of herself except in relation to her mother; she was dependent on her and so her instinct was to embrace her, to radiate her with love and affection. As we get older we become more self-dependent, more aware of our own abilities and less aware of our dependency on God. Because of that I think that we are less inclined to recognise moments of grace, to be surprised at things. My own memory of growing up as a child was that I became less inclined to hug my mother, more self-conscious, more aware of my own independence. It is something I regret. To be open to someone else's love is to be child-like, to be dependent, but in the end, it is to be free. The acceptance of unconditional love from a parent, or from God, and to respond to that love is probably one of the most difficult things we will ever have to do as adults. But grace is abundant if we can learn to accept love. When we love another person in freedom, when we accept the spontaneous love of another person and allow ourselves to be 'scooped up', we can embrace that person, and that moment, in complete freedom and happiness.

But God loved us with so much love that he was generous with his mercy: when we were dead through our sins, he brought us to life with Christ – it is through grace that you have been saved – and raised us up with him and gave us a place with him in heaven, in Christ Jesus. This was to show for all ages to come, through his goodness towards us in Christ Jesus, how infinitely rich he is in grace. Because it is by grace that you have been saved, through faith; not by anything of your own, but by a gift from God; not be anything you have done, so that nobody can claim the credit. We are God's work of art, created in Christ Jesus to live the good life as from the beginning he had meant us to live it (Eph 2:4-10).

Like a mother for her child God loves us and is infinitely rich in his grace. Grace is a gift from God, something unmerited but which should evoke in us a response, a turning towards God and our neighbour in an embrace of love. To refuse that free gift of love is to prefer the darkness to the light as John tells us in his gospel:

> On these grounds is sentence pronounced:
> that though the light has come into the world
> men have shown they prefer
> darkness to the light
> because their deeds were evil.
> And indeed everybody who does wrong
> hates the light and avoids it,
> for fear his actions should be exposed;
> but the man who lives by the truth
> comes out into the light,
> so that it may be plainly seen that what he does is done
> in God (Jn.3:19-21).

A KINGDOM DIVIDED AGAINST ITSELF

The Tenth Sunday in Ordinary Time, Year B

One of the most marvelous and intimate books of poetry I have read for some time was the collection of poems, *Newborn* by Kate Clanchey. The book charts and articulates the roller-coaster of human emotions of a mother from the conception of her child through the first years of its new life. The collection begins with the author looking at a photograph of herself caught in a church doorway leaning down to fasten her sandal strap. She remembers that the church stood at a confluence of rivers and even remembers their names:

> I've even noted their names,
> And the date, which says you, love,
> Are perhaps ten cells old.

As she bends down she is intimately aware of the presence within her and speaks as if to the child:

> …You / are putting me on, easily,
> The way a foot puts on a shoe.[15]

The poet / mother addresses the child as if the child was at the centre, determining the mother's place in the world. It is the child who 'puts on' the mother, the child who is the foot putting on her shoe, her mother. The whole relationship between mother and child is turned around so that it is the child who is at the centre. I remember the first time I read those poems and the sense of exhilaration I felt, the sense of revelation. It was as if the medium of poetry had revealed with such an economy of words, what theology might take a life-time of manuals to struggle to say. And this was accessible, intimate, true to a poet's experience. There was no logic, no deduction from first principles, just a truth revealed in a moment, an instant, the way a sudden rainbow might affirm our faith in the beauty of the world, in the majesty of God. It strikes me that there might be something of the priest in the poet and the poet in the priest. Both attempt to straddle two worlds, to make sense of our lives lived in the here and now and how they fit into a more eternal world. In *Sacred and Secular Scriptures – A Catholic Approach to Literature*, Nicholas Boyle says this: 'We have only to pick up a new volume of Seamus Heaney, or for that matter an old volume of Dickens, or even Pope, to have revealed to us a truth at which the reason of the Deists could not arrive before the end of the world.'[16] This is not to make an extravagant claim for literature or to suggest that if literature does 'reveal' something to us that it is necessarily religious. In fact, one imagines that a novelist or a poet might be deeply offended by the meaning of his/her work being 'hi-jacked' for a religious dogma or point of view. It is simply to suggest that literature does reveal much about the human condition and that is precisely what those of us who call ourselves 'religious' should be interested in. It is also to suggest, in a modest way, that poets, novelists, playwrights, musicians and artists have borrowed and continue to borrow much from the 'religious' traditions. Religion or faith, properly understood, opens up to all of us other worlds, new dimensions, more subtle ways of seeing things. In an age of increasing materialism and fragmentation all of us need to be continually renewed by the 'marvellous' in life. Perhaps as a Church, when we moved away from the old rituals, we lost some sense of the marvellous and the mysterious in our liturgies. And yet I think that we can recover that by tapping into and relating the marvels of the sacraments to contemporary expressions and experiences of the marvellous – in poetry, in music, in art and in nature. There is no doubt that there is a deep sensitivity in the Irish make-up to the artistic, the aesthetic. There appears to be a renewed interest and keenness for the arts and a spirituality that springs and grows from an appreciation of nature, the creation of God. This is perhaps best articulated and celebrated in the work of John O'Donohue whose intuitive approach to spirituality has attracted many. It may be that some of us in the institutional Church have lost our pull on the imagination of many and the danger here is that we view the growth in an alternative spirituality as threatening. There is an equal danger that an imagination which frees itself from the rituals of tradition might relegate the sacramental life of the Church to a past time. There is need for a space where creativity and sensitivity in the arts and in alternative spiritualities can be in dialogue with a more traditional approach to revelation and the sacraments long revered in the Church.

Both develop our understanding of our place in the world, both articulate something fundamental about the human condition. In a poem or a piece of music, a Celtic meditation or the Way of the Cross we come closer to understanding who we are as pilgrims in this world, members of the kingdom of God.

> The scribes who had come down from Jerusalem were saying, 'Beelzebul is in him,' and, 'It is through the prince of devils that he casts devils out.' So he called them to him and spoke to them in parables, 'How can Satan cast out Satan? If a kingdom is divided against

itself, that kingdom cannot last. And if a household is divided against itself, that household can never stand.' (Mk 3:22-25).

The kingdom of God is built up in many different ways from the traditional rituals of the Church to the marvellous revelations of poetry, literature and human encounter and experience. The scribes were protective of their authority and saw anyone who cast out devils, not in their name, as a threat. Often we as a Church are overly protective of the kingdom and we feel threatened by different spiritualities and expressions of faith.

But the kingdom of God finds expression both in the Church and in the world of which the Church is an important part. We might find the kingdom in the surprise of a poem's final stanza or in a Celtic meditation just as we might find it in the sacrament of reconciliation or the sacrament of the Eucharist. When we relegate a poem or a painting to something that is merely secular, we limit the many ways in which God's kingdom finds expression in our world. We threaten to divide the world between the sacred and the profane, as if all creation is not a wonderful manifestation of God's presence, as if the Word had not become flesh.

THE SIGN OF THE CROSS

The Fourth Sunday of Lent, Year A

As children we were taught the importance of blessing ourselves when passing a church. Both my mother and grandmother made sure that we showed appropriate respect when passing a church because a church was the house of God, the place where Christ was present in the tabernacle. I've never forgotten that lesson and even today, almost unconsciously, I bless myself when passing a church. There was something in it, something that I suspect is lost on many of the younger generation today. It recognised the church as special, as a place apart, a sacred space to be acknowledged, however modestly. Years later, during the Troubles, when individuals took 'refuge' in a church I had little difficulty in understanding it as a place of sanctuary.

A few years after my ordination, while sitting at traffic lights in the centre of Derry, I watched a young man hold on to a bottle of vodka with one hand and to the railings of the cathedral with the other. I recognised him from my old primary school; he was a few years older than me and I knew that he had had a drink problem for some time. Months before I stopped to speak with him in the city centre after he asked me for money. I remember the sadness I felt when he called me 'Father' because we had been to school together, although then we only knew each other to see. I felt sorry because I wondered what had happened in his life and in my own that set us on two very different paths. Here we were not even twenty years on, and our lives seemed so different. Or were they really that different, I wondered? Perhaps the fact that I still had both my parents alive, that I had had more opportunities to further my education, and had some kind of clear goal in life, perhaps these held together a self as fragile and vulnerable as his was broken and painful? That's why I felt sad when he recognised me as a priest and not as someone who went to the same school and played in the same streets. Is life really that accidental, I wondered, really that fragile, that two young boys could become two very different men? Were we two very different men or were we similar? What vulnerabilities and weaknesses did I disguise in my efforts to fit into society's caricature of a priest? He told me that his mother had died and how he had broken her heart because of his drinking. His father had died years before. He cried bitterly about his mother, about her love for him, and his inability to show gratitude for it. We spoke for some time that day and I tried to tell him that we grew up together and went to the same school but it didn't make sense. I suspect that very little made sense anymore. I tried to make sense of it myself but couldn't.

It was with all of this in mind that I saw him again holding on to the railings of the cathedral. I thought of our conversation a few months before and of his mother. And then, as he swapped the bottle of vodka from one hand to the other, steadied himself against the railings and blessed himself, I was reminded of my own mother and how she had taught me to do the same. I began to feel that damp haze clouding over my eyes as I watched this most beautiful act of faith, in the context of such human brokenness and desolation. I wondered had his mother taught him that just as my mother had. Suddenly I saw the whole meaning of that simple lesson we had learned as children. It rooted us to something profound, something sacred, something redemptive when everything else falls apart. I thought of a passage from Graham Greene's *The Power and the Glory* where the 'whisky priest' gives into despair and accumulates in secret '...the rubble of his failures. One day they would choke up, he supposed, altogether the source of grace.'[17] I thought of how the sign of the cross, that most fundamental of all Christian gestures, might stop us from choking up, finally, the source of grace. I thought, too, of another passage from John's gospel when Jesus heals a blind man who used to sit and beg:

> They brought the man who had been blind to the Pharisees. It had been a sabbath day when Jesus made the paste and opened the man's eyes, so when the Pharisees asked him how he had come to see he said, 'He put a paste on my eyes, and I washed, and I can see.' Then some of the Pharisees said 'This man cannot be from God; he does not keep the sabbath.' Others said, 'How could a sinner produce signs like this?' And there was disagreement among them. So they spoke to the blind man again, 'What have you to say about him yourself, now that he has opened your eyes?' 'He is a prophet' replied the man.
> 'Are you trying to teach us,' they replied 'and you a sinner through and through, since you were born!' And they drove him away (Jn 9:13-17; 34).

The Pharisee is in each one of us when we drive people away and marginalise them. The Pharisees felt morally superior to the blind man in the story because they believed that his blindness was a punishment from God for sin. His sinfulness confirmed their righteousness and sense of superiority. It is a temptation that many of us who profess to be 'religious' in the sense that we 'practise' our faith are open to. There is a great temptation in any Christian society to set up a divide between the virtuous and the sinner, thereby denying the reality of sin in all our lives and the possibility of redemption that is offered to each of us. A passage from the first book of Samuel, where God is choosing a King, reminds us that God looks at each of us differently. The Lord says to Samuel, 'Take no notice of his appearance or his height for I have rejected him; God does not see as man sees; man looks at appearances but Yahweh looks at the heart' (1 Sam 16:7).

THE WORLD WILL BE SAVED BY BEAUTY

The Nineteenth Sunday in Ordinary Time, Year A

Grianan of Aileach is one of the most spectacular stone forts in Ireland. The word 'Grianan' is the old Irish word for a 'sunny place' and its definition easily attaches itself to the fort in County Donegal for it sits splendidly on a hill-top between the valleys of the Foyle and Swilly rivers with panoramic views of Counties Donegal, Derry and Tyrone. Visible from my sitting-room window, I can drive to the fort in about fifteen minutes.

In an entry under the year 1101, The *Annals of the Four Masters* records that the fort was demolished by Murtagh O'Brien, King of Munster, at the head of the forces of Leinster, Ossory, Meath and Connaught. From the historical sources, we know that Aileach was the seat of the O'Loughlin kings of the northern Ui Neill dynasty, whose title 'Aileach' distinguished them from other members of the Ui Neill. The fort, at one time, may have housed the 'palace' of the Kings of Aileach. Whatever about the history of Grianan of Aileach, its beauty is incontestable. It is approached by turning left off the main road from Derry to Letterkenny at the Church of St Aengus at Burt, a beautiful church modeled on the fort, the design of which led to a prestigious award for the Irish architect Liam McCormick. A narrow winding road leads from the church up to the stone fort and the ascent is marked by increasingly beautiful panoramic views of the surrounding countryside. The last hundred yards to the fort are made on foot and once inside the visitor can climb a series of terraced steps to the top of the fort where a whole world is revealed and the sense of open space is overwhelming. I remember Grianan from my childhood as a special place. My parents occasionally took us there on Sundays, where from an old well, attributed to St Patrick, we carried small bottles of holy water home. We used to climb inside the small low chambers that were located on either side of the east-facing lintelled entrance passage. Without knowing much about the history of the place we knew that this was special; we sensed in the cold stone that we stood on another time, long before our own, when this was someone's home, when these stones were someone else's defence. In the breeze that caught the heather and pushed itself through the small lintelled doorway we felt a freedom, a freshness, a refreshing of ourselves, a stretching out of summer when school was closed and we had no worries. Fifteen minutes from home, we felt as if we were a thousand miles away.

Today Grianan of Aileach remains a sacred place for me, not because of the apocryphal story of St Patrick's well that we were told as children, but because of the place itself, of what it manifests in its magnificence, what it opens up in its freedom. I associate it now more with my own past than with its own, more with my carefree childhood than the cares of medieval Kings. Whenever I am troubled or upset I make the small journey to it as a place of pilgrimage, a place where I can continue to stand in the fresh air gliding off the heather, refreshing my spirit, reawakening my gratitude for its beauty, for the world's beauty, for the grandeur of God. Grianan provides a context, a vista, within which and from which I can see my place, my joys and sadness, my goodness and my frailty as part of a bigger picture, of a more beautiful world where everything dissolves in the breeze around me and for once I am me again, uninhibited by oppressive spaces within myself and in the immediate world around me. I want to offer prayer in thanksgiving. Here is beauty before me, the tangible presence of something beyond me, an absolute, a revelation unattainable by reason. I feel as if I need to give something back, to respond to this gift, to carry away some of that gentle heather-touched breeze within me and allow it to freshen the lives of others.

In his Nobel Lecture in 1970 Alexander Solzhenitsyn began his lecture by reflecting on Fyodor Dostoyevsky's remark in *The Idiot* that the world will be saved by beauty. He wondered how beauty had the capacity to save our world from lies and violence. His conclusion was that beauty is a manifestation of truth and that not even lies can stand up forever against the enduring goodness and beauty of art.[18] Solzhenitsyn reflects on beauty in the context of art and literature, but the same claim might be made for beauty in the context of the natural world. Surely art, at one level, seeks to represent the innate beauty of the world around us. The created world is a profound manifestation of God's presence, a revelation of God's own beauty. The concept of beauty as a theological aesthetic, and of Christ as the revelation of beauty-glory, was most explicitly reflected on in the work of the theologian Hans Urs von Balthasar.[19] Beauty, in the natural world around us, beauty in art and in literature does have the capacity to open up for us a space where in freedom we can recognise God's presence and our relationship to Him in profound humility and thanksgiving. It should come as no surprise that Christ so often prayed in 'lonely places'.

Mountains are often places of prayer in the Old and New Testaments. In the first book of Kings we are told that the prophet Elijah reached Horeb, 'the mountain of God' and went into a cave and spent the night there. On Horeb, Elijah finds the Lord in a gentle breeze:

He [Elijah] walked for forty days and forty nights until he reached Horeb, the mountain of God. There he went into the cave and spent the night in it. Then he was told, 'Go out and stand on the mountain before Yahweh.' Then Yahweh himself went by. There came a mighty wind, so strong it tore the mountains and shattered the rocks before Yahweh. But Yahweh was not in the wind. After the wind came an earthquake. But Yahweh was not in the earthquake. After the earthquake came a fire. But Yahweh was not in the fire. And after the fire there came the sound of a gentle breeze. And when Elijah heard this, he covered his face with his cloak and went out and stood at the entrance of the cave (1 Kgs 19:9, 11-13).

All three synoptic gospels tell us that Jesus himself sent the crowds away so that he could pray by himself: 'He [Jesus] made the disciples get into the boat and go on ahead to the other side while he would send the crowds away. After sending the crowds away he went up into the hills by himself to pray' (Mt 14:22-23).

If we continue to encounter the Lord on hills and in the natural beauty around us and if it moves us to prayer, to gratitude, and to goodness, then perhaps the world will be saved by beauty.

THE HOSPITALITY OF CHRIST

The Body and Blood of Christ, Year A

The Supper at Emmaus is, perhaps, one of the most beautiful paintings by the Renaissance artist Michelangelo da Caravaggio. It depicts the recognition of Christ by the two disciples during supper. The depiction of the disciples as common labourers with weathered faces and shabby clothes would have struck people of the seventeenth century as irreverent and even outrageous. Caravaggio insisted on painting scenes from the Bible, truthfully and faithfully, as he understood them. The great art critic Ernst Gombrich said of him that he wanted to see the holy events '...as if they had been happening in his neighbour's house'.[20]

I fell in love with the painting as a young A Level art student. Five years later, in the summer of 1994, when I went to see the painting in the National Gallery in London, I felt the excitement of a little boy who has waited patiently for something he has always wanted. When I located the painting on the guidebook I walked with eyes downcast, not wanting to see any other painting until I had seen *The Supper at Emmaus*. I was a little nervous as though I were witness to a minor epiphany. I would see the face of Christ as Caravaggio himself had seen it in his mind's eye, and as he had handed it on in canvas through a powerful gesture of creation and generosity. When I found the room I scanned it quickly until I saw the painting hanging there, much larger than I thought. I walked over to it and stood before it like some altar, some place where Christ is made present. I was startled and disorientated by the way

I felt. I couldn't decide if I was happy or sad. I felt my eyes well up with tears and, in a moment of absolute forgetfulness, I almost knelt down before it. I felt a strange sense of belonging, a sense of welcome, as if Caravaggio had painted this for me. I was reminded of a beautiful remark by the literary critic George Steiner when he talked about the 'hospitality of art'.[21]

I found it difficult to describe my experience when I stood before that painting except by way of comparison. I remembered falling in love for the first time as a teenager and how the feeling seemed almost too much to bear, too much happiness and sadness in the one moment. Now as I reflect on that time I realise that I was happy that I should be given an experience so beautiful, sad that I could never hold on to it. I remembered being told that after long months of treatment for cancer my seven-year-old sister Jacqueline, would live. I remembered watching the sun set over Lough Swilly and wanting to cry out how grateful I was to be alive. All I could do as I stood before that painting was to compare that experience to those others in my life. What it meant at the time I didn't know except that it meant something, something beyond words, something beyond that moment, something beyond even the painting itself. I felt as if I couldn't contain the joy of it, that my heart or soul would burst if I tried to possess it and that suddenly here again was a link between joy and sadness.

Today I would define all those moments as moments of grace. Grace itself I would define as an unmerited gift from God. The gift of the real presence of the Body and Blood of Christ, celebrated in Caravaggio's painting, is the most profound moment of grace. It is the most profound moment of presence where we live in Christ and Christ lives in us:

> I am the living bread which has come down from heaven. Anyone who eats this bread will live for ever; and the bread that I shall give is my flesh, for the life of the world… He who eats my flesh and drinks my blood lives in me and I live in him (Jn 6:51, 56).

That 'hospitality' of Christ allows us to live with each other in the hospitality of community that St Paul talks about in his letter to the Corinthians:

> The blessing-cup that we bless is a communion with the blood of Christ, and the bread that we break is a communion with the body of Christ. The fact that there is only one loaf means that, though there are many of us, we form a single body because we all have a share in this one loaf (1Cor 10: 16-17).

I believe that our experience of the real presence of Christ in the Eucharist is complemented by other moments of presence before someone we love, before a painting, before a sunset. And perhaps the sadness we sometimes feel in moments of great joy is a reminder that we do not live on bread alone but on everything that comes from the mouth of the Lord. God humbles us and makes us feel hunger for something more:

> 'Remember how Yahweh your God led you for forty years in the wilderness, to humble you, to test you and know your inmost heart – whether you would keep his commandments or not. He humbled you, he made you feel hunger, he fed you with manna which neither you nor your fathers had known, to make you understand that man does not live on bread alone but that man lives on everything that comes from the mouth of Yahweh (Deut 8: 2-3).

The sense of loss or sadness we feel in moments of profound beauty or happiness is a reminder that our final contentment is in union with Jesus Christ. The presence of Christ in a painting, in someone we love, in a sunset, is finally fulfilled in the gift and grace of his own Body and Blood.

THE SPIDER'S WEB

Christmas Day, Year B

On my way to work each morning I walk a narrow garden path down to a green gate, beyond which are the grounds of the school. There are times of the year when it is more attractive than others. In the early spring some of the flower beds are full of daffodils, the stalks of which are tied together as they fade before the onset of summer. The hawthorn trees are pregnant with stippled florescent green which gives way to a heaviness with the fullness of summer. Summer brings its own colours and smells, its own sweetness before the hibernation of autumn sets in and winter pauses growth and life. Like many other people I find winter hard and I feel in myself something of the barrenness all around me. I find fewer surprises in winter, fewer scented smells, fewer colours and insects, fewer epiphanies or awakenings to the beauty of the world around me. I find prayer more difficult in winter, perhaps because I see less of the grandeur of God that charges the world around me. Not even time survives winter, for it cuts the days in half.

There is, however, one particular beauty attached to winter that re-awakens me. For weeks, during one particular winter, I walked down the short garden path and through the green gate to school unaware of a beauty that threaded itself from the top of a garden post to an adjacent stone wall. It was only with the colour of a hard winter frost that I saw the magnificent spider's web come to life. It must have been there for weeks, spun as I walked past carelessly, unaware of this marvellous pattern. I stopped to look at it, to study it, to be in awe of it. Each silken thread, fragile in itself, and spun together in a beautiful pattern of symmetry and strength, a strength that could carry a winter's frost. I marvelled at it, marvelled that I hadn't seen it until a night's frost made its beauty crystal clear. I wondered what it meant, what it pointed to, what it stood for. That it was a moment of grace I knew, but that it might define something of the mystery of grace I reflected on later.

On Christmas Eve I had been stopped by a teenager in a busy shopping centre who asked me to hear his confession. He was standing with a group of friends and there was nothing irreverent in his request, however surprising I found it. He was troubled and worried, something of a lost soul who in that moment and that place wanted to talk, to confess, and receive the forgiveness of God. Something touched him, someone touched him in that moment and that unlikely place. Something touched me – his witness, his courage, his humility; in the middle of the chaos in a shopping centre I was suddenly aware of a presence, of a touch, that affected both of us, a touch, on reflection, that I believe was the winter touch of God. I thought of the fragile threads of his life, of my life, that held us together, that could be destroyed at any moment by the carelessness of life. I thought of grace as God spinning the fragile threads of our lives into a pattern and into a strength. I thought of grace becoming tangible, of this wonderful feast, of the Word becoming flesh:

> In the beginning was the Word:
> the Word was with God
> and the Word was God.
> He was with God in the beginning.
> Through him all things came to be,
> not one thing had its being but through him.
> All that came to be had life in him
> and that life was the light of men,

a light that shines in the dark,
a light that darkness could not overpower...
The Word was made flesh,
he lived among us,
and we saw his glory,
the glory that is his as the only Son of the Father,
full of grace and truth (Jn 1:1-5; 14).

The feast of Christmas celebrates the touch of God, his humanity, his presence in the world, his grace. Faith is difficult, like the winter darkness. We search for signs, for growth before the day closes and the darkness sets in. Sometimes when our prayer is barren we want to touch something, to be touched by something, to bring colour to that which we cannot see. I've often wondered why so many people who don't go to mass on a regular basis, or at all, come to mass on Christmas Day. I used to think that some sense of tradition brought them. But I've come to believe that for many people at Christmas the presence of God in family, in kindness and in reconciliation, is tangible. I believe that at Christmas, some people discover grace, a grace that has always been there, a grace brought to life by the winter touch of God.

St Paul in his letter to the Hebrews tells us that God speaks to us through his Son, the winter child we celebrate on this feast. Christ is our light that shines in the dark, a light that darkness cannot overpower.

'At various times in the past and in various different ways, God spoke to our ancestors through the prophets; but in our own time, the last days, he has spoken to us through his Son, the Son that he has appointed to inherit everything and through whom he made everything there is' (Heb 1:1-2). Christ is our light that shines in the dark, a light that darkness cannot overpower.

How beautiful on the mountains,
are the feet of one who brings good news,
who heralds peace, brings happiness,
proclaims salvation... (Is 52:7).

THE POSTCARD

The Eighteenth Sunday in Ordinary Time, Year B

I never thought that a postcard could bring such comfort to a widowed woman who had just lost her son in a tragic accident. The wake house was remote, in County Donegal, not far from a convent of nuns, tranquil except for the tragic news of Jimmy's death. He had been home from England just a week before, as he was frequently, to see his mother and catch up with the rest of the family. His mother loved his visits and fussed over him as if he were still a child and hadn't flown the nest of home years before to look for work in England. Leaving each time to go back was almost as sore as the first time, certainly for his mother. Each time he left, the request was always the same, to send a postcard back home and keep in touch. This he did, faithfully. The last postcard he sent home was similar to all the others; he thanked his mother for a lovely time at home and wrote at the bottom of the card, 'You are the best mum in the world. I love you, Jimmy'. On his way home from posting the card Jimmy walked along the beach. It was here, it seems, that he fell and hit his head and drowned in a small pool of water. When the local police eventually identified him they contacted his family with the shocking news. Only a week before, he was home and fine, already looking forward to his next visit. The family suspended their grief and got the house ready for his last return home. In the mornings after his death his mother collected cards of sympathy from the local postman; they tried to reassure her, offer her comfort and prayers, and they were welcome. But one card, although it broke her heart, she handled as if she were receiving the consecrated host itself; Jimmy's last postcard told her that he had returned safely, thanked her for the holiday, and told her that he loved her. The postcard was to become the most treasured possession she had, a tangible memory of him, his handwriting proof of him, its sentiments, the presence of him.

I remember Jimmy's mother taking out the postcard from her bedside locker and showing it to me at his wake. There was something remarkably strange about the presence it evoked of the same man who was waked in the room we stood in. There was almost something more real, more authentic about the small piece of card that I held than the body over which I prayed 'Eternal rest...' It was late in the evening when I got home and when I made the connection between the postcard and the Eucharist as the ultimate gift of love. Both the card and the bread are worthless in themselves but something transforms them, transfigures them, transubstantiates them so that they take on the presence of a loved one, the presence of the Divine one. I wouldn't want to push the analogy or attempt to 'explain' the mystery but I found the grace of the postcard an encouragement in deepening my awareness of the grace of the sacrament. I have found it a useful analogy in teaching about the idea of real presence, since so often today, presence is understood as a physical, verifiable thing, in the sense that we set out to prove the existence or non-existence of 'ghosts', for example.

In John's gospel, the people ask Jesus what sign he will show them that they should believe in him. They refer to the story in Exodus where the Israelites in the desert were given manna from heaven. Christ answers them:

I tell you most solemnly,
it was not Moses who gave you bread from heaven,
it is my Father who gives you bread from heaven,
the true bread;
for the bread of God
is that which comes down from heaven
and gives life to the world.
'Sir,' they said 'give us that bread always.' Jesus answered:
'I am the bread of life.
He who comes to me will never be hungry;
he who believes in me will never thirst' (Jn 6: 32-35).

All of us yearn for presence, for the presence of another to love us, reassure us, make us complete. The hunger that we feel, the deep desire for contentment and wholeness, arises out of our incompleteness, our need for relationship. And even with human relationships and presence we still find ourselves yearning for more, for another presence that is the source of all our deepest and most profound desires. The 'manna' of human relationships does not finally fulfill our hunger; we still cry out for food that will last, for love that will fill the deepest vacuum in our spirit. The Eucharist, Christ present in the bread and wine, is the source of our final peace, the true bread of God, which has come down from heaven and gives life to the world.

'BETTER TO LIGHT A CANDLE...'

The First Sunday of Advent, Year C

In 1961 a British lawyer called Peter Benenson was shocked to read in the newspapers about two Portuguese students who had been sentenced to seven years in prison for raising their glasses in a toast to freedom. Deciding that he could not ignore such blatant injustice he placed an appeal in a newspaper entitled 'The Forgotten Prisoners' which was published worldwide on 28 May 1961. His appeal brought in more than one thousand offers of support for the idea of an international campaign to protect human rights. Within twelve months the new organisation had sent delegations to four countries to make representations on behalf of prisoners, had taken up over two-hundred cases, and had organised national branches in seven countries. The organisation became known as Amnesty International and an image of a candle enclosed in barbed wire remains the symbol of the organisation – it was inspired by the Chinese proverb, 'It is better to light a candle than to curse the darkness.' The general aims of Amnesty are to promote general awareness of human rights and to oppose specific abuses of human rights throughout the world. Amnesty promotes awareness of human rights by encouraging all governments to ratify and enforce international standards of human rights and also by carrying out a wide range of education activities. Examples of human rights abuses that

Amnesty focus on are torture and other cruel, inhuman or degrading treatment or punishment, the use of the death penalty by governments, the 'disappeared' – people who have been taken into custody by government authorities or by armed political groups, but whose whereabouts and fate are kept secret – deliberate and arbitrary killings, the detention of prisoners of conscience, and children taking part in armed conflict.

My involvement with Amnesty International over the years has encouraged me to reflect on the place of human rights, and active involvement in seeking to prevent human rights abuses, in the context of the Christian faith. It seems to me that there is a direct correlation between the call of the gospels to liberate the captives and free the oppressed and Amnesty's call to free prisoners of conscience and those who suffer from torture and other degrading treatment. Amnesty does not need to espouse any particular faith or religion for a practising Christian to see the organisation as one way in which he or she can build up God's kingdom on earth and live out the call of the gospels. That a practising Christian should also pray for those who are oppressed and invoke the power of God to free captives is self-evident and is not threatened by an organisation that, for good reason, does not affiliate itself to any particular faith or religion. It also seems important to me that the work of Amnesty parallels the social teaching of the Roman Catholic Church, which is especially encouraged by Pope John Paul II.

St Paul in his letter to the Thessalonians prays that the community will love not just each other, but the whole human race:

> May the Lord be generous in increasing your love and make you love one another and the whole human race as much as we love you. And may he so confirm your hearts in holiness that you may be blameless in the sight of our

God and Father when our Lord Jesus Christ comes with all his saints (1 Thes 3:12-13).

The theme of social justice is particularly evident in the Old Testament prophets. Jeremiah talks about King David practising 'honesty and integrity in the land' (Jer.33:15). The fulfillment of such honesty and integrity is finally realised in the second coming of Christ when Christ will bring our liberation (Lk.21:28). Until the second coming of Christ and the full realization of God's kingdom of truth, love, justice and peace on earth, those of us who are Christians must find ways of setting captives free, restoring sight to the blind and breaking the oppressor's rod. Amnesty International is one very practical way of giving expression to our Christian faith.

THE DIGNITY OF LIFE

In every child born and in every person who lives or dies we see the image of God's Glory.

Pope John Paul II, *Evangelium Vitae*

THE VIA CRUCIS

Good Friday

It was only in recent years that I visited the Colosseum in Rome despite having studied and taught Roman history long before that. I visited it in April during Holy Week. The day was damp but mild and all around the Colosseum men were selling umbrellas, water-colour prints of Rome, and cheap mementos of the ancient city. Despite the intrusiveness of some of those selling their merchandise, there was something civilized about the whole thing, couples sitting lost in the 'romance' of the place, artists trying to define the scale of the monument, and others just taken in and aback by the history around them. I joined the long queue to go inside the arena; I wondered was it worth the wait in the light rain to see what I could squint at through the stone arches at eye level. In the end the queue moved faster than I thought and within twenty minutes I was inside the arena. On reflection I'm glad that I waited because nothing that I had experienced outside the vast stone circumference could have prepared me for how I felt inside those walls. It was as if the stories I had read in Tacitus and other Roman historians had come hauntingly to life. I felt a chill that was absent outside, a guilt at having praised for years this wonderful piece of architecture that must have seemed like the gates of hell once to the many who entered it. Despite obvious differences, I thought about the gate into Auschwitz. Was it the magnificence of the architecture and the past 'glory' of Rome that allowed people to admire this place where glory was built on slavery, where death was presented as entertainment, and where human life was valued even less than that of the exotic animals that were such an attraction in the place? People didn't admire Auschwitz in the same way. The Colosseum was different to the Forum or the Palatine Hill; this was an arena of death where someone else's suffering was someone else's fun.

It was as if in that one place the suffering in the world today had been collected in my own mind. I thought of the modern arenas of death, from Auschwitz to the Sudan, from Rwanda to Latin America. I thought of those enslaved in our own modern 'civilized' world, children used in pornography and women brought from foreign countries and forced into prostitution. I wondered how hypocritical it was to talk of the barbarity of the Romans when so much of our own entertainment is derived from the exploitation and abuse of other vulnerable human beings. I decided that the Colosseum stands not as a reminder of the inhumanity of the ancient Romans but of our own, two thousand years on. Only inside that arena did I finally understand the full significance of the Via Crucis celebrated in Rome on Good Friday every year.

Each year the Christian community of Rome, together with pilgrims from around the world, gather at the Colosseum on the evening of Good Friday to celebrate the Stations of the Cross. Millions of people take part through television in this moment of contemplation and prayer. They are united around the mystery of the passion and death of Christ, following the way of the cross from inside the Colosseum to the slopes of the Palatine Hill. The reflections on the Stations seek to link the mystery of Christ's suffering with the contemporary suffering of millions of people throughout the world today, people who suffer as a result of poverty, neglect, abuse, exploitation, violence, persecution and warfare. The photos of thousands of faithful people carrying candles in the darkness surrounding the Colosseum are a powerful reminder of Christ who is the Light of our darkened world. The Colosseum becomes no longer an arena of death but a space where light is made possible and hope made visible. The drama that unfolds in that sacred space in Rome is enacted and re-enacted in churches throughout the world, where suffering is shared and faith professed.

Christ turns the ancient spectacle of death around so that now we, as spectators, are appalled at his suffering:

> ...As the crowds were appalled on seeing him – so disfigured did he look that he seemed no longer human... Like a sapling he grew up in front of us, like a root in arid ground. Without beauty, without majesty (we saw him), no looks to attract our eyes; a thing despised and rejected by men, a man of sorrows and familiar with suffering, a man to make people screen their faces; he was despised and we took no account of him.
>
> And yet ours were the sufferings he bore, ours the sorrows he carried. But we thought of him as someone punished, struck by God, and brought low. Yet he was pierced through for our faults, crushed for our sins. On him lies a punishment that brings us peace, and through his wounds we are healed' (Is 52: 14; 53: 2-5).

I could only make sense of my visit to the Colosseum in the light of the Via Crucis, in the light of this as a space for hope rather than a place of despair. It is as if the ritual of Good Friday attempts to make sense of the suffering endured there in much the same way as Greek Tragedy attempted to make sense of something unbearable and despairing. It turns it around so that light can be thrown on it, the light of Christ who is forever the Light of the World.

THE OPEN DOOR

A Reflection On Suicide

One of the fondest memories of my childhood was when my mother or father put me to bed. I remember, clearly, my mother saying, 'I'll leave the door open and the landing light on.' The shaft of light that came through the narrow open space was enough to ensure that the darkness was never total. I remember doors as things that kept the heat in and the cold out; they allowed friends in and kept strangers out, and they let the light in and kept the darkness out.

That particular memory of childhood rises up in my mind when I learn of the tragic death of a young person by suicide. I imagine the sense of total darkness, the overwhelming sense of fear. I think of doors, of the doors closed to these young people in life, of the doors they close to themselves out of fear, of the doors of their homes through which they leave for the last time. I was particularly struck by the significance of doors at the funeral of a relative of mine who took his own life. I remember returning from the morgue with his family and seeing from one end of the street the wide open door of his family home. I was suddenly struck by that space, that threshold, at once a leave-taking and home-coming, both a door out into the dark and a welcome home into the light and warmth of family.

Do not let your hearts be troubled.
Trust in God still, and trust in me.
There are many rooms in my Father's house;
if there were not, I should have told you.
I am going now to prepare a place for you,
and after I have gone and prepared you a place,
I shall return to take you with me;
So that where I am
You may be too (Jn 14: 1-3).

It's no coincidence, I think, that heaven should be presented as a home. The image is warm and recognisable. We like to think that our loved ones return home to a familiar place, a place of welcome. The idea of Christ preparing a place for us is as human and reassuring as a mother preparing her daughter's room after her first term away from home at university. My own abiding memory of my return home from Maynooth was the warmth and tidiness of my own bedroom; without ever saying it I knew that my mother had spent time cleaning it, in expectation of my homecoming. In a mother's or father's love for a child we catch a glimpse of God's infinite love for us. A parent's love is unconditional, accepting and reassuring. But Christ goes even further; after preparing a place, a room, for those whom he loves he returns to take them home. Christ is present not only for someone's return but for their journey. Often when someone dies we worry about their journey, about fear lasting beyond the grave, but in John's gospel we are assured that Christ accompanies our loved ones to the door of paradise.

When a young person takes their life our whole 'programmed' understanding of death and its place in the cycle of things is thrown into turmoil. The death of someone young manages, somehow, to reverse the cycle of life. We expect to bury our parents and when we do, we close a door to the past. With the death of a young person the cycle of life is turned round and we close a bridge to the future. And that is the tragedy of a young person's death – that life's promise and potential remain unfulfilled. The tragedy is that something precious has been taken from us and we are the poorer for it.

The tragic death of someone young, especially in the circumstances of suicide, has a profound impact on their peers and their friends. The unexpected and unexplained nature of suicide jolts young people, startles them and brings the remote and almost unthinkable possibility of death onto their own doorsteps. No-one will deny the complexities and the sadness that can often accompany growing up. Young people meet with disappointments in life, as all of us do, but their mechanisms for survival are much more fragile, less tried and tested by life's broader experiences. That is why it is so important that they keep the doors of their lives ajar. Often, when a young person meets with sadness they retreat into a room of darkness and bolt the doors of their lives from the inside so that even those who might have the keys to unlocking their sadness cannot get in. In my experience of parents and families who lose a loved one in the tragic circumstances of suicide, I find that they carry with them so many unresolved questions. They wonder why they didn't see it coming, how they could have prevented it, why their son or daughter could not feel their love. But I think that in this context the image of the door is a helpful one. Once a child or a teenager locks their pain and hurt in a room and bolts the door of that room from inside, then not even the unconditional love of a parent can unlock the door of sadness from outside. There is less stability for children and teenagers than there was in the past and so it is even more important that we search for ways of shining light into their lives, if only to keep the darkness from becoming complete.

A beautiful poem by Patrick Kavanagh comes to mind, 'To A Child':

> Child do not go
> Into the dark places of the soul,
> For there the grey wolves whine,
> The lean grey wolves.
>
> I have been down
> Among the unholy ones who tear
> Beauty's white robe and clothe her
> In rags of prayer.
>
> Child there is light somewhere
> Under a star,
> Sometime it will be for you
> A window that looks
> Inward to God.[22]

There is much that can steal the light from the lives of young people today. Parents and teachers, and all who work with young people in a special way, have a responsibility to shine light into their lives, to create a window that looks 'inward to God'.

'I WAS A STRANGER...'

The Feast of Christ the King, Year A

Oksana Sukhanova was only twenty-seven years old when she lost both her legs to frostbite. That she lost them at all was a tragedy; that she lost them not in the poor and unforgiving climate of her homeland, the Ukraine, but in the 'hospitable' and relatively prosperous modern Ireland, was shocking. Just before Christmas she had lost her job and had been sleeping rough on the streets in bitterly cold weather. She was found on New Year's Day in a terrible condition. She was taken to the Causeway Hospital and then transferred to the Belfast City Hospital where surgeons amputated both her legs. Later she was moved to Musgrave Park Hospital where she was fitted with two prosthetic limbs.

It was early in the New Year when I heard the story of Oksana Sukhanova on the news. I was suddenly stopped in my tracks; here was a young woman who lay out on the streets over Christmas, not even fifty miles from where I lived, and froze while I ate and drank more than I should have in the warmth and luxury of my family home. This was too close to home, too real and tangible to imagine that I could have done nothing to prevent it. This was not suffering in some remote impoverished part of the world, this was here in my own country, right under my nose, in the full glare of Christmas lights celebrating the birthday of Christ our King. This was the real Christmas story, the need for an inn, for shelter, for some small expression of love, and all of it in the context of a Christian community that reflects nostalgically on the Christmas crib. On 6 January, I looked at my own crib differently from when I had put it up before Christmas. It was as if it had come to life and was gazing back at me critically, implicating me in its asylum and isolation. Two thousand years of distance from the human tragedy of a pregnant mother with nowhere to stay had turned the crib into one more decoration, as glittering and shallow as the fairy lights on the Christmas tree. Over the years the cold isolation of that first nativity scene had become the warm, nostalgic community of the Holy Family with shepherds, kings and kindly animals. Little wonder that Christ, present in a refugee freezing to death on a doorstep, was missed. That this was a truer and more tragic reflection of the first Christmas was lost on me because I misunderstood the crib as confirmation of my warm idea of Christmas, rather than a criticism of it.

The story of Oksana Sukhanova shocks even more because it happened at Christmas, when over-indulgence is greater and even the most hardened of us feel some sense of guilt at our excesses. But suffering and poverty on that scale are with us the whole year round in the homeless, in refugees, asylum seekers and those suffering from terrible addictions. Despite the promise of a booming economy, the gap between rich and poor continues to exist and it seems that the bigger our houses get, the smaller our doors become – open doors, doors of welcome, doors into the warmth and out of the cold. Wealth, even relative wealth, creates distance. The more secure we become, the less we are able to empathise or even sympathise with those who have nothing. Money is seductive, the more we have the less we are inclined to share. It was the ultimate downfall of the rich young man in the gospels.

There was another reason why I felt so disturbed personally by the plight of Oksana Sukhanova. On my ordination prayer card in 1997 I had borrowed a line from chapter 25 of Matthew's gospel as my 'creed' for my priesthood. The line comes from Matthew's famous depiction of the last judgement, when Jesus says to his disciples:

> 'When the Son of Man comes in his glory, escorted by all the angels, then he will take his seat on his throne of glory. All the nations will be assembled before him and he will separate men one from another as the shepherd separates sheep from goats. He will place the sheep of his right hand and the goats on his left. Then the King will say to those on his right hand, 'Come, you whom my Father has blessed, take for your heritage the kingdom prepared for you since the foundation of the world. For I was hungry and you gave me food; I was thirsty and you gave me drink; I was a stranger and you made me welcome; naked and you clothed me, sick and you visited me, in prison and you came to see me.' Then the virtuous will say to him in reply, 'Lord, when did we see you hungry and feed you; or thirsty and give you drink? When did we see you a stranger and make you welcome; naked and clothe you; sick or in prison and go to see you?' And the King will answer, 'I tell you solemnly, in so far as you did this to one of the least of these brothers of mine, you did it to me.' (Mt 25:31-40)

Like the crib at Christmas, the last line of that story which I chose as my creed for priesthood is at the same time my encouragement and my own judgement. It remains my greatest challenge and the challenge of all of us who profess our faith in Christ the King to see in our suffering brothers and sisters the face of Christ we so instantly recognise in Christmas cribs.

Moth In Waterloo

The Thirteenth Sunday in Ordinary Time, Year A

During the summer holidays I spend some time working in a parish in Kingston-upon-Thames just outside of London. While there I avail of the opportunity to travel around London and enjoy some of the musicals in the West End. Waterloo Bridge is impressive and there's little doubt that London is a breath-taking city by night. Walking towards Waterloo station, Saint Paul's floodlit cathedral sits almost in the centre on the left, with Westminster on the right, dwarfed only by the London Eye.

Some years ago I walked across the bridge to the subway, which leads eventually to Waterloo station. It was just after half past ten and I was hoping to catch the last train to Kingston. The underground and underworld of the subway are in stark contrast to the lights and glamour of the city. It's an underground of hidden despair and desperation. I walked past three people in sleeping bags. They didn't speak but held out polystyrene cups, rigidly, as if they were mime artists in Covent Garden. Presumably they had grown weary of asking people for money and sat there poised in despair. I walked past the first two convincing myself that I might miss the train and that if I stopped with one I would have to stop with everyone. It was easier to blend into the crowds which were rushing past to catch their trains. I felt bad but it was still easier to walk on. As I approached the third person I looked up and saw a young teenage girl. She caught me looking at her and so I found it difficult to walk on. It is easier to walk past a person when you haven't looked into their eyes; something fails to connect. To look into someone's eyes, however, is to connect if only for a moment, and suddenly the despair and hopelessness are real and to walk on would be to deny that person's humanity. I did stop this time and reached into my pocket and gave her two pounds. She thanked me and I said 'you are welcome' and walked on.

If I felt bad at having ignored two people who were homeless, I felt worse for having patronised a third. Why had I given her money, for her benefit or for my own? What was her name and when was the last time anyone called her by it? How had she ended up on the streets? Did she have a family, a mother and a father? When was her birthday? When was the last time someone said that they loved her? Did she love herself? Why hadn't I asked her those questions? I decided that I had given her money not that she might enjoy a good night's sleep but that I might.

I did catch the last train back to Kingston and sat on a seat near a window. As I sat down I noticed a huge moth just inside the window. I felt uncomfortable and got up and sat across on the other side. As I got up a young well-dressed man, with a briefcase, got on the train and sat on my original seat. I paid little attention to him until he got up from his seat and turned towards the moth on the window. He shaped his hands into a cup and slowly and gently lifted the moth from the glass. He walked over to an open window and, again, gently put his hands outside, opened them, and allowed the moth to fly out into the darkness of Waterloo station. I should have felt uplifted but I didn't. I felt sad and I turned towards my own window and my eyes welled up. The girl on the subway steps had probably not experienced such gentleness for years.

There's a beautiful story in the second book of Kings when the prophet Elisha is shown wonderful hospitality as a stranger. A woman at Shunem builds a small room for the prophet and in a beautiful reciprocal gesture the prophet promises her a son:

> One day as Elisha was on his way to Shunem, a woman of rank who lived there pressed him to stay and eat there... She said to her husband, 'Look, I am sure the man who is constantly passing our way must be a holy man of God. Let us build him a small room on the roof, and put him a bed in it, and a table and chair and lamp; whenever he comes to us he can rest there (2 Kgs 4: 8-10).

When Elisha asks his servant what he can do to repay the woman's hospitality, his servant Gehazi tells him that the woman has no son and that her husband is old:

> Elisha said, 'Call her.' The servant called her and she stood at the door. 'This time next year,' he said 'you will hold a son in your arms' (2 Kgs 4: 16).

The theme of welcome for the stranger is most explicitly stated by Christ himself in Matthew's gospel:

> Anyone who welcomes you welcomes me; and those who welcome me welcome the one who sent me. Anyone who welcomes a prophet because he is a prophet will have a prophet's reward; and anyone who welcomes a holy man because he is a holy man will have a holy man's reward (Mt10: 40-41).

Paul reminds us in his letter to the Romans that we suffer a death in baptism:

> ...When we were baptised in Christ Jesus we were baptised in his death; in other words when we were

baptised we went into the tomb with him and joined him in death, so that as Christ was raised from the dead by the Father's glory, we too might live a new life (Rom 6: 3-4).

Death to selfishness must be a fundamental part of our journey in faith if we are to extend to our fellow human beings the kindness we show easily to moths and animals.

The Bird's Nest

The Fourth Sunday of Advent, Year C

It was as at the age of eight that I experienced a breach of trust from a school friend. We grew up two streets apart just above a field we used to play in after school. One of the fondest memories I have of that field comes from the mid-winter when there was a fall of snow and a few of us would sleigh down it, sitting on top of an old biscuit tin lid. I remember it as a freezing cold day but at least the memory is warm. The other memory I have of that field was from a warm spring day but, for all the warmth of that day, the memory remains a cold one.

I made a small discovery in the spring of 1979. A few of us were playing in the field after school. One of us threw a ball in under a hedge and I went to get it. Not very high up in the hedge I could see this small bird's nest with three tiny eggs in it. I was genuinely moved at this little wonder and at their mother who flew back and warmed them as I left. Despite the excitement I felt I was reluctant to tell the others and so after school every day I would come to the field on my own to see if the little family had hatched. I probably had a better understanding then of Advent as a time of waiting, than I do now as an adult. I would never get too close but from a distance would watch the mother sitting still as the protector of her unborn family.

On the way back from the field one day I met my friend from school who asked me what I was doing there on my own.

Although we were friends I wouldn't have trusted him with a little family of eggs. My friend knew that I was hiding something and begged me to tell him. When he made all sorts of promises I decided to expose this little unborn family. I remember what happened then as one of the most formative experiences of my childhood. When I showed him the nest he teased me about it and he moved closer and closer so that the mother reluctantly flew off. She didn't fly very far but watched from the safe distance of another tree. My friend tore the nest from the tree and dumped the eggs onto the ground. I begged him to put them back but instead he stood on the three eggs until they were destroyed and suddenly for me the marvellous had turned into the murderous.

I often wondered why God chose to come into the world in the way that he did? Why go through the nine months of growth in the womb before birth? The answer I think is that to deny that nine months to the Son of God would have been to deny the sacredness of that time between mother and unborn child. It would have been to deny the marvel and wonder of those nine months, what Seamus Heaney called in one of his poems, a 'consecration.'[23]

> Mary set out and went as quickly as she could to a town in the hill country of Judah. She went into Zechariah's house and greeted Elizabeth. Now as soon as Elizabeth heard Mary's greeting, the child leapt in her womb and Elizabeth was filled with the Holy Spirit. She gave a loud cry and said, 'Of all women you are the most blessed, and blessed is the fruit of your womb' (Lk 1: 39-42).

The child in Elizabeth's womb leaps for joy when Mary greets Elizabeth. It's one of the most moving passages in the gospel of Luke. And it's a reminder to the secular world we live in that life is not a commodity to be purchased or discarded but is a gift of the most profound sacredness. We are living in an age where the commercialism that attaches itself to Christmas threatens to attach itself to children. Mothers, pregnant with a child that will be severely disabled, are offered the option of abortion. That is the reality that we face in a world that has become obsessed with the importance of the individual.

The message of Christmas needs to be heard more than ever in today's world and that message is that a child was born into the world to redeem all of us from our own selfishness and to remind us that life is a gift from God. When my friend stood on those eggs he betrayed a trust that I had placed in him. God has entrusted us with his creation and with the gift of each other. I believe that unless we embrace the message of Christmas in a radically new way, embrace the profound dignity of every human person, including the unborn child, we will have betrayed the trust of the infant Son of God.

THE CRADLE OF TRUST

The Feast of the Holy Family, Year C

It is only now as an adult that I appreciate the family environment that I was brought up in. When I say 'family' I refer, first and foremost, to my immediate family, my parents and brothers and sister. As an extended part of that 'blood' family were my aunts and uncles and cousins, all of whom were in contact at various times to a greater or lesser extent. But there was a further family again, not in any blood-line, but closer by proximity and contact, and that was the local, tight-knit community in which I grew up as a young boy and teenager. Even now I can recall with fondness almost every name of those who lived on either side of the street I grew up on. At the top of the street was an open field where we could play safely and live as if we were a million miles from home; at the bottom of the street, just two houses below our own, was a row of shops that was the hub of the community, the centre around which conversation turned and a whole fabric of society and day to day life was weaved, strengthening itself without even knowing it. In her later years, my grandmother became preoccupied about saving money, for her funeral, as she very candidly put it back then. She would send me with a very modest list of 'messages', as we called it, to a local shop run by a very kind man called Davey. When I would return I was quizzed about the price of a packet of biscuits and if my grandmother thought they were too expensive then I was sent back to return them and get her money back. I used to be humiliated and wait until the shop was quiet and then explain to Davey that my grandmother thought his biscuits were too expensive. He used to give me some change and tell me to take the biscuits back and ask my grandmother if that was okay. When the first really big supermarket came to Derry when I was a teenager I thought it was great, a symbol of progress. On reflection, I doubt if it would have extended my grandmother the same privilege.

So I situate my own immediate family in that wider context because it was a thread in the fabric, in the same sense that every other family were threads that pulled together and defined a wider family, a whole community focused around a field and shops. And the security that I felt at home with my parents and younger brothers and sister was reflected in the security of good neighbours, in people I could trust. As a child I took all of it for granted, my family and the people who made up my own local community.

I go back a few times a year to visit an old neighbour, Mrs Coyle, who was kind to me as a small boy; she was my next door neighbour. Along with my parents and my grandmother she was influential in my decision to study for the priesthood at eighteen. I find it hard going back to the street because it threatens to demolish or tarnish my memories of it. My family home is now rented out to students and the curtains remain closed in it even during the day. I think sometimes that it is a good thing that I cannot see inside to the room we kept good for the Christmas tree and the open fire. Directly opposite my old home, my grandmother's house appears the same, curtains pulled and the brass on the door that I had so faithfully polished every week, turned dark, the sparkle gone. Some of the neighbours have died and most of the others have moved away. Davey retired a number of years ago from the shop.

My memory of family and community life is of course a nostalgic one but the small sense of desolation that I feel when I return to the place where I grew up touches another experience far more immediate and relevant. The sense of family, of community that I remember from those times is being gradually eroded not just in that place important to me, but in society as a whole. There is a real sense of disintegration, of things falling apart, as families break down and the fabric that holds a wider community together threatens to unravel at an enormous pace. I wouldn't want for a moment to suggest that my own experience of family or community was perfect. Undoubtedly there was lots going on in families that we didn't know about but by and large the family unit of two parents and children remained a kind of building block for the wider community. I wouldn't want to suggest either that the reasons for family breakdown are straightforward or are the same in all cases. For every family that runs into problems and breaks down there are individual circumstances and individual people who are hurt. Every story is different and every story is painful.

So how do we talk about family in these difficult and fragmented times? We need to acknowledge first of all where we are at as a society and as a community. From my own experience as a teacher there is little doubt that family breakdown adversely affects children; the more I talk to children who have been affected by the separation or divorce of their parents the more I see the hurt that it causes. This is not a judgement but a statement of fact. Children need security and division within a family threatens that. In his book *The Politics of Hope* the Chief Rabbi Jonathon Sacks says the following:

> We know more than this, namely that the family is the crucible of much that matters in later life, the growth of sympathy and trust and sociability. It is where we acquire our identity, self-confidence, responsibility, attachment, fellow-feeling, the moral sentiment itself. It is where we learn who we are, where we came from, and where we belong...We, individually and collectively, are the

guardians of the world of trust, and the family is its birthplace.[24]

While being sensitive to the terrible pain for everyone involved when a family breaks down, we must also strive to preserve the integrity of the family in an effort to provide for our children an environment that nurtures community, forgiveness and patience. I don't think that it is too naïve to suggest that we can still look to the Holy Family, who suffered their own difficulties, as a model towards which we can set our sights:

> Every year his parents used to go to Jerusalem for the feast of the Passover. When he was twelve years old, they went up for the feast as usual. When they were on their way home after the feast, the boy Jesus stayed behind in Jerusalem without his parents knowing it…Three days later they found him in the Temple, sitting among the doctors, listening to them, and asking them questions…They were overcome when they saw him, and his mother said to him, 'My child, why have you done this to us? See how worried your father and I have been, looking for you.' 'Why were you looking for me?' he replied. 'Did you not know that I must be busy with my Father's affairs?' But they did not understand what he meant. He then went down with them and came to Nazareth and lived under their authority. His mother stored up all these things in her heart. And Jesus increased in wisdom, in stature, and in favour with God and men (Lk 2: 41-43; 46; 48-52).

There is much that we as a society need to store up in our hearts so that we can begin the process of healing required to bring us together again as a family.

RECONCILIATION

We must learn to live together as
brothers or perish together as fools.

Martin Luther King, *Speech at St Louis*

THE FAR SIDE OF REVENGE

The Twelfth Sunday in Ordinary Time, Year C

John Plummer was a helicopter pilot during the Vietnam War and in 1972 he helped to organise a napalm raid on the village of Trang Bang. The full horror of that particular bombing came to light because of an award-winning photograph of a nine-year-old girl running toward the camera, burned and naked with her arms outstretched and billows of black smoke rising behind her. Phan Thi Kim Phuc captured, in her desecrated and outstretched body, the brutality and inhumanity of warfare. In an image that became one of the twentieth century's icons of the human cost of war the figure of the nine-year-old girl could have been lifted straight out of Picasso's *Guernica*. The image disturbed John Plummer in particular; he had been behind the bombing and although he had tried to clear the village of civilians it hadn't worked and now he faced the full horror of what he had done in the tortured image of a young girl. He wanted to go back and say that he was sorry, to find the girl whose burned body threatened to haunt him for the rest of his life. An unexpected chance to put things right came on Veteran's Day 1996 when John attended the Memorial in Washington, DC. Twenty-five years on Kim had also come to Washington to face her own very hurtful past. She spoke to the crowd about her own forgiveness for the people who had bombed her village and who had hurt her so badly. John Plummer's moment had arrived to face his past and say sorry.

After Kim had finished speaking he made his way towards her and identified himself as the pilot who had bombed her village. It must have seemed as grave as the day of judgement, as dramatic as Damascus. Kim recognised John's pain, his tortured efforts to come to terms with his past; she held out her arms and embraced him. John Plummer, who twenty-five years before had caused such hurt, said again and again that he was sorry. Kim reassured him that it was okay and that she forgave him. At another meeting Kim reassured him again of her forgiveness and from that chance meeting they kept in touch by telephone. Kim had found the strength and the grace to forgive and John had found the healing and forgiveness he needed to move on.[25]

The story has an immediate resonance for me with the aftermath of the bombing in Enniskillen in 1987. In the aftermath of that terrible massacre there were rumours that Loyalist paramilitaries were intent on revenge but that the words of forgiveness from Gordon Wilson, who had lost his daughter Marie in the bombing, encouraged a less violent reaction. A devout Methodist, he said that he prayed for those who had murdered his daughter. He later met with members of the IRA to ask them, in the name of all the innocent people who died in the Troubles, to declare a ceasefire; his appeal fell on deaf ears but his prophetic witness to the importance of forgiveness and reconciliation in his own life has touched the lives of many in Northern Ireland and beyond. As a young teenager I was hugely touched by the life and witness of Gordon Wilson, by the cross he was asked to carry. I thought of his loss and pain, his own injuries and the terrible loss of his twenty-year-old daughter who held his hand under the rubble as she was dying. I thought of Christ's instruction to his disciples:

> 'The Son of Man' he said 'is destined to suffer grievously, to be rejected by the elders and chief priests and scribes

and to be put to death, and to be raised up on the third day.' Then to all he said, 'If anyone wants to be a follower of mine, let him renounce himself and take up his cross every day and follow me. For anyone who wants to save his life will lose it; but anyone who loses his life for my sake, that man will save it' (Lk 9: 22-24).

Forgiveness is, in the end, an act of faith, reaching out beyond a cycle of hate and revenge towards another horizon, a horizon perhaps more easily understood only after huge personal suffering. It is inexplicable in human terms, something beyond reason and logic, something brought about by emptying oneself of hurtful pride and reaching out towards another, an enemy, in complete love, a love that transcends all hurt and pain. Few ever achieve the monumental gestures of Phan Thi Kim Phuc or Gordon Wilson but their acts of forgiving love prompt us, nudge us towards reconciliation in our own lives, towards healing and forgiveness. They show us another possibility, a way out of retaliation and revenge, a horizon beyond the barren shores of instant revenge and summary justice.

In Seamus Heaney's version of Sophocles' *Philoctetes* Heaney explored the way in which victims of violence can themselves become slaves of their wounds and how there is need in the end for belief in other possibilities. In one of the most celebrated passages of that play, Heaney has the chorus say:

> So hope for a great sea-change
> On the far side of revenge.
> Believe that a further shore
> Is reachable from here.
> Believe in miracles
> And cures and healing wells.[26]

ACHILLES AND PRIAM

The Seventh Sunday in Ordinary Time, Year A

Homer's *Iliad* recounts the events of a short part of the tenth and final year of the epic war between the Greeks and the Trojans. Its subject is the 'wrath of Achilles' arising from an affront to his honour given by Agamemnon, leader of the Greek army at the siege of Troy. Although it recounts only a small part of the war, in effect, it encapsulates the whole war, with the final death of the Trojan hero Hector, symbolising the fall of Troy that will soon follow.

Early in the story Achilles, offended by Agamemnon, withdraws to his tent from the fighting. For most of the story he nurses his grievance and even when Agamemnon offers to make amends for the damage he has caused, Achilles refuses to fight for the Greeks. As the Greeks continue to suffer losses at the hands of the Trojans, Achilles grants permission to his friend Patroclus to assist the Greeks in battle and lends him his armour to fight. In the battle that follows Hector, son of the Trojan King Priam, kills Patroclus. Achilles, on hearing the news, vows to avenge the death of his friend. Maddened with grief, Achilles puts aside his anger with Agamemnon and rejoins the Greeks in battle. With new armour fashioned by the god Hephaestus, Achilles sets out to murder Hector. As Achilles races towards the gates of the palace at Troy, Hector's parents beg him not to fight Achilles alone. Hector himself is afraid but he feels that he has brought about his own fate and so he goes out to meet Achilles. As Achilles approaches and grabs him, Hector loses his courage and turns and runs in fear. Homer recounts the story with great pathos and sympathy liking Hector's fleeing to an eagle's prey running in terror, sure to be cut down. As Hector finally faces Achilles, he asks him to agree to allow him the proper funeral games if Achilles should slay him; Hector promises this to Achilles should he fall. Achilles, however, consumed by hatred refuses Hector's request. When Achilles drives his ash spear through Hector's throat he is not content with his dying. He tells him that he will leave his body to be mauled by the dogs and birds. With his dying breath Hector begs him to give his dead body back to his parents but Achilles says no. When Hector dies Achilles treats his body with gross outrage, tying it by the heels to his chariot and dragging it through the dust, in front of his distraught parents.

Towards the end of the book, Hector's father, King Priam, immersed in suffering and sadness for his son, comes to Achilles' tent to beg him for the return of his son's body. It is one of the most beautiful passages in classical literature. Priam asks Achilles to remember his own father at the 'cruel edge of old age' and what he would feel if he heard that Achilles had been killed and his body mutilated. At the mention of his father – Achilles is moved to pity and when Priam curls up at his feet both of them weep together, Achilles for his own father and Priam for his murdered son. Achilles calls his servants to wash and anoint the body of Hector before he gives it back to Priam, wrapped, to carry home to Troy. After they had eaten together, Priam returned home with the body of his son.[27]

Long before I read Homer's *Iliad*, at the age of seventeen, I watched on television the murders of corporals Derek Wood and David Howes in West Belfast. The killings came in the wake of a gun attack by Michael Stone at the funerals of three IRA members killed by the SAS in Gibraltar. Three people were killed by Stone at the funeral. It was unclear how the soldiers managed to get caught up in the funeral of one of Stone's victims but it seems that some thought that this might be another attack at a republican funeral. The images of what followed have stayed with me ever since and haunted me as a teenager. The soldiers were dragged from their car and punched and kicked to the ground. They were then dragged to nearby Casement Park where they were beaten again, and stripped to their underpants and socks. The two badly beaten bodies were then taken away in a black taxi to waste ground where they were shot and stabbed a number of times. The Redemptorist priest Father Alec Reid knelt beside the two dead soldiers and administered the last rites; the picture remains one of the most enduring of the troubles. Derek Wood's mother died when he was twelve and his grandmother who raised him watched on television unaware that one of the soldiers was her grandson.

Later, when I read the *Iliad*, I cried at the death of Hector because I thought of those two soldiers. I thought of their parents and grandparents watching the barbarity of their deaths, as Priam watched the death of his son from the walls of Troy. I thought of Derek Wood's father flying to Northern Ireland to bring the dead body of his son home for burial, just as Priam had done.

In 1994 when the IRA declared their ceasefire, the Belfast poet Michael Longley wrote a poem called 'Ceasefire' based on that final scene between Achilles and Priam in the *Iliad*.[28] He didn't draw any explicit parallels but allowed the story of that reconciliation between a Trojan King and a Greek warrior to say something to us about the need for reconciliation and healing, almost three millennia later.

> 'You have learnt how it was said: Eye for eye and tooth for tooth. But I say this to you: offer the wicked man no resistance. On the contrary, if anyone hits you on the

right cheek, offer him the other as well…You have learnt how it was said: You must love your neighbour and hate your enemy. But I say this to you: love your enemies and pray for those who persecute you; in this way you will be sons of your Father in heaven, for he causes his sun to rise on bad men as well as good, and his rain to fall on honest and dishonest men alike (Mt 5: 38-39, 43-45).

There is much to be done by way of reconciliation and healing in Northern Ireland, but a story from ancient Greece shows us possibilities, other ways of responding to cycles of violence and hate. To step out of the cycle, to step out for a moment from the straitjacket of our history and to empathise with those who share our suffering is to make all things possible in a new society.

THE BELL

The Seventh Sunday in Ordinary Time, Year B

The Bell by Iris Murdoch, tells the story of a lay-community encamped just outside Imber Abbey, the home of an enclosed order of nuns. Many members of the lay-community have had disastrous relationships in life and they are there hoping to find salvation through prayer and through sharing their stories with each other in the abbey. But the community itself gradually disintegrates through the moral weaknesses and sexual flaws of its members. When Michael, the leader of the community, becomes painfully aware of his own human weaknesses and failures as a person, he decides to confess all his mistakes to Sister Clare, the old Abbess. Michael has become obsessed with his own failures and with his misguided love for another member of his community. He pours out his heart to this old nun who listens to everything he has to say. When he finishes, Sister Clare says to him, 'Remember that all our failures are ultimately failures in love. Imperfect love must not be condemned and rejected, but made perfect. The way is always forward, never back.'[29]

I am reminded of the story when I read the following passage from Isaiah:

> No need to recall the past,
> no need to think about what was done before.
> See, I am doing a new deed,

even now it comes to light; can you not see it?
Yes, I am making a road in the wilderness,
paths in the wilds...
I it is, who must blot out everything
and not remember your sins (Is 43:18-19. 25).

It is probably one of the most liberating passages in the Old
Testament. There is a real sense in which all our failures in life
are ultimately failures in love. The man or woman who is
unfaithful to their partner; the priest who is unfaithful to his
ministry; the teenager who overdoses because of a failed
relationship; the young girl of six who hides under the bed
sheets so as to drown out the noise of her parents fighting.
Failures in relationships, failures in love threaten to overwhelm
us so much so that we see no way out except to indulge in self-
pity and crippling guilt. But the good news of Isaiah is that we
are not slaves to past failures, we are not condemned to a life
half lived where we fail to love others because we cannot love
ourselves. Sin paralyses us; the weight of it enslaves us. We
become shadows of our true selves, forever attached to our
past. Interestingly in the New Testament Christ often forgives
people before he heals them:

> When he [Jesus] returned to Capernaum some time
> later, word went round that he was back; and so many
> people collected that there was no room left, even in
> front of the door. He was preaching the word to them
> when some people came bringing him a paralytic carried
> by four men, but as the crowds made it impossible to get
> the man to him, they stripped the roof over the place
> where Jesus was; and when they had made an opening,
> they lowered the stretcher on which the paralytic lay.
> Seeing their faith, Jesus said to the paralytic, 'My child,
> your sins are forgiven' (Mk 2:1-5).

Later in the story Christ cures him of his paralysis. It is sin that paralyses us, that makes us unwell. Imperfect love must not be condemned and rejected, but made perfect. The way is always forward, never back. At the end of *The Bell*, Sister Clare encourages Michael to have faith in God and to remember that God, in his own time, will complete what we so poorly attempt. Often our failures are the result of a love that is selfish or immature; only God can purify our love through his redeeming grace. We must not become prey to despair; we must not allow our weakness to drag us down to a barren place where the love of God is starved of growth. There is no need to recall the past; God is doing a new deed, making a road in the wilderness.

WOUNDING THE HEART OF CHRIST

The Sacred Heart of Jesus, Year B

In the year 2000 the National Gallery in London hosted an impressive exhibition called *Seeing Salvation* in which the image of Christ and how it evolved over two millennia was explored.[30] The exhibition traced the changing image of Christ as recorded by various artists, from the earliest symbolic and metaphorical images such as the Shepherd, the Lamb and the Vine, through to the 'true likeness' of Christ inspired by the image of Christ on the cloth, allegedly held out to Jesus on his way to Calvary. In that exhibition, images of Christ's suffering during the Passion were intended to convey not just an historical moment in time but something about the universality of suffering, something that could connect with our own experience of suffering, both personal and communal, in the twenty-first century. Christ's Passion was offered to us not just as an individual's suffering but as a continuing reflection of all human suffering. It was both a reflection *of* that suffering and *on* that suffering so that we might better understand our contemporary experience, both as Christians and non-Christians, in the light of this archetypal moment when the Son of God suffered his Passion.

In one part of the exhibition a comparison was made between fifth-century images depicting the Passion and Resurrection of Christ and a thirteenth-century image representing the Virgin and Child, and Christ as the *Man of*

Sorrows. Despite their similarity of theme they are as different as the two different centuries were in which they were created. One of the fifth century images represents Christ's crucifixion and Christ is depicted as almost superhuman; his body is muscular and perfectly upright against the cross which is hardly visible and his head is held high with his eyes wide open. Opposite, Judas hangs ignominiously from a tree, the pieces of silver spilling from his pouch onto the ground. There is no doubting Christ's Divinity even as he hangs on a cross. The contrast, eight centuries later, with Christ as the *Man of Sorrows* is stark and revealing. It reveals Christ, not in his Divinity but as a suffering human victim, a man of sorrows whose mother shares his pain. The *Man of Sorrows* icon is also known as the '*Imago Pietatis*' (Image of Pity) because it is both a depiction of passion and an invitation to the viewer to share in Christ's suffering, to be compassionate. Gradually in Western art a special emphasis came to be placed on the humanity of Christ and on his Passion.

What I like about the thirteenth-century image is the way in which it invites us to share in the sufferings of Christ while at the same time reminding us of the part we continue to play in his Passion. It involves us not just as spectators but as people who participate in Christ's suffering. The image is at once for us and against us, iconic of our own personal suffering and chastising of the suffering we inflict on others. In its humanity we can conjure up our own men and women of sorrows eight hundred years on who are crucified because of exploitation, poverty, injustice and violence. They invite our compassion and pity just as Christ the *Man of Sorrows* does, but they also implicate us as perpetrators of injustice who remain silent while they continue to suffer. They are living witnesses to Edmund Burke's judgement that all it takes for evil to thrive is for good people to do nothing. We are implicated not because of what we do but because of what we don't. Often family loyalties, political sympathies or religious allegiances keep us from standing up for what is the truth, from speaking out and actively seeking to end someone else's suffering. Brian Moore, in his novel *Lies of Silence,* depicted a society torn apart by violence where it was better to stay silent than speak out against injustice.[31] It is not at all easy to stand up for what is right but each time we allow someone to suffer in silence we wound the heart of Christ:

> It was Preparation Day, and to prevent the bodies remaining on the cross during the sabbath since that sabbath was a day of special solemnity – the Jews asked Pilate to have the legs broken and the bodies taken away. Consequently the soldiers came and broke the legs of the first man who had been crucified with him and then of the other. When they came to Jesus, they found he was already dead, and so instead of breaking his legs one of the soldiers pierced his side with a lance; and immediately there came out blood and water... Because all this happened to fulfil the words of scripture: 'Not one bone of his will be broken'; And again, in another place scripture says: 'They will look on the one whom they have pierced' (Jn 19:31-34; 36-37).

Christ as the Man of Sorrows continues to evoke pity and compassion in a world of injustice and violence. He is as much an icon for our times as when he was first depicted eight hundred years ago and he continues to draw us to 'look on the one whom they have pierced' so that we share not just in his suffering but in his mission to bind up all wounds.

EPIPHANY

The Feast of the Epiphany

I've always found the last few days of the year and New Year's Eve, in particular, to be difficult. Maybe it's the fact that it marks some kind of passing and seals a year's joys and sadness, to be folded away in the storeroom of memories we call life. I find the new year fine and welcome its newness and promise, but until I have passed over that threshold between one year and the next I seem tied to the year gone by, stock-taking its produce, for good and for bad. I felt particularly melancholic towards the end of the last millennium and the beginning of this one. Perhaps the hype that surrounded the transition to 2000 had something to do with it. There are times also when I reflect back on a year of my life and regret mistakes I have made, people I have hurt, and apologies I never got round to making. It's as if at the end of the year they come back as ghosts waiting to be laid to rest before I can move on and move in to another year. I felt like that on the eve of 2000. But I felt something else too. My brother and his wife were waiting for their twins to be born. Deirdre went into labour on 30 December and gave birth to twin boys later that night. My mother phoned me late that evening to tell me the news. I found that night a strange place to be, in-between the regrets of one year and the sheer wonder of the next, torn between human failure and divine grace, between the frailty of two tiny new-born boys and my own frailty as an adult. I couldn't make sense of it and so I sat down to write, to articulate an overwhelming feeling of strangeness.

The following day was New Year's Eve and I drove to the hospital to see the twins. I brought two miraculous medals, two teddy bears and flowers for Deirdre. When I went into the ward my brother Keith was holding one little boy and Deidre the other. They were tiny. Keith passed one of the twins to me and told me to mind his head. I was shocked at the lightness of his weight, this fragile little being completely dependent on others. His eyes were squinting in the light, his tiny fingers open wide. I felt like crying as I held him, felt as if nothing came purer than this, nothing more sacred. This was a surprise moment, an epiphany of sheer joy, a moment of redemption. Here in my arms was the antidote to failure, the promise of hope, a moment of grace. I felt uplifted, felt as if these twin boys in their wonder and lightness, pointed towards something, towards a grace I was hungry for. Later I reflected on that beautiful passage from Isaiah:

> Arise, shine out Jerusalem, for your light has come,
> the glory of Yahweh is rising on you,
> though night still covers the earth
> and darkness the peoples.
>
> Above you Yahweh now rises
> and above you his glory appears.
> The nations come to your light
> and kings to your dawning brightness
>
> Lift up your eyes and look round:
> all are assembling and coming towards you,
> your sons from far away
> and daughters being tenderly carried.

At this sight you will grow radiant,
your heart throbbing and full;
since the riches of the sea will flow to you;
the wealth of the nations come to you... (Is 60: 1-5).

I thought of the light that both Fearghal and Aodhan had already brought into our lives as a family. I watched them as they were tenderly carried by their father. Like Isaiah I felt radiant in their presence:

'The sight of the star filled them with delight, and going into the house they saw the child with his mother Mary, and falling to their knees they did him homage' (Mt 2: 11).

My own small act of homage was to write this poem for Fearghal and Aodhan:

Epiphany – 30 December

for Fearghal and Aodhan

With what love I learned
of your incarnation
on that damp night
with Christmas spent
and the New Year in labour.

My heart heavy with failure
I drove to pay you homage.
A teddy bear, miraculous medal
and flowers, I bore my gifts
only to receive, in some double-take
yours.

'Mind his head,' Keith said,
passing this little weight across,
his eyes straining to the light
of a new world.

I forgot for a moment
where I had been
and what I had left behind.
In your lightness I learned again
wonder – that your helplessness
could restore a fallen world.

You, who were my epiphany,
revealing, manifesting
grace and truth,
stirring, re-creating anew my world
you who were twinned
in the womb of your mother.

WHY THE WORM?

The Twenty-Sixth Sunday in Ordinary Time, Year B

In *The Book Against God* by James Wood, the narrator, Thomas Bunting, articulates the story of his own complicated and deceitful life. In the opening chapter he tells us that he has been neglecting his PhD and concentrating instead on another project, the writing of a book he calls *The Book Against God*, or *BAG* as he refers to it. His marriage is falling apart and he has a somewhat awkward relationship with his father, an Anglican parish priest. As well as being a confirmed atheist, Thomas Bunting is also a chronic liar. Throughout the novel he lies repeatedly to his father who is a sincere man, apprehensive about where his son stands on the question of God. When his marriage is in trouble he comes to live with his parents and hopes to be able, finally, to communicate honestly with his father. Towards the end of the novel, in order to please his father, he tells him that he is seeking something, seeking God, he thinks. His father is delighted, relieved that his son has at last found the reason for the void in his life, a void he has been filling with alcohol. His father smiles at him, pleased at his new found faith. In the end Bunting's 'searching' turns out to be the final lie a son will tell his father. Shortly afterwards the father dies of a heart attack. At the end of the novel Bunting clings to tenuous memories he has of his father, to the time his father held his hand at his grandmother's funeral. He talks to his dead father in the final paragraph where he recalls the happiness of his childhood:

> When anyone asks me, I say that my childhood was happy, and for once, for once, I am not lying. Wasn't it an orchard, my childhood? But why, then, the worm? Why the worm? Tell me.[32]

My own father used to regale us, as children, with stories of how he and his friends used to raid orchards when they were children. It was a simple, if prohibited, pleasure, he told us, when there was little else for children to do. Since they couldn't bring their stolen goods home they would eat them and share them with other friends. Occasionally, he remembered, biting into some rotten fruit, something rotten from the inside out, something made rotten by a worm. I remember almost being put off eating fruit as a child and even today I still cut through apples with a knife, just in case.

That image of my father raiding orchards in the height of summer, on the one hand, and biting into rotten fruit, on the other, has stayed with me as an adult. It was as if it was a precursor to something other than goodness, a metaphor for what we later understood as adults to be original sin:

> And if your hand should cause you to sin, cut it off; it is better for you to enter into life crippled, than to have two hands and go to hell, into the fire that cannot be put out. And if your foot should cause you to sin, cut it off; it is better for you to enter into life lame, than to have two feet and be thrown into hell. And if your eye should cause you to sin, tear it out; it is better for you to enter into the kingdom of God with one eye, than to have two eyes and be thrown into hell where their worm does not die nor their fire go out (Mk 9:43-47).

The reference in Mark to the worm that does not die is taken from the prophet Isaiah where Yahweh talks of how all the nations that he will gather to himself will endure:

> And on their way out they will see
> the corpses of men
> who have rebelled against me.
> Their worm will not die
> nor their fire go out;
> they will be loathsome to all mankind (Is 66:24).

The metaphor of the worm in Isaiah, borrowed by Mark, is one of death caused by sin. The prophecies of Eldad and Medad in the book of Numbers and of James in his 'answer for the rich' (Letter of St James, 5:1) are echoed again in Christ's prophecy in Mark's gospel. Throughout the ages prophets have resisted evil and have manifested the Spirit of God in their lives. As we leave childhood and its securities we become aware of the many choices we must make for ourselves. We become aware of selfishness, of its capacity to consume us to a greater or lesser degree. We become embroiled in the complexities of other people's lives, the complexities of our own. We have some sense in which our childhood too was an orchard, of moments when we took our parents' hands and followed them wherever they took us. As adults we might not have the hands of our parents to hold us but we believe, in faith, that God, through the promptings of the Holy Spirit, guides our way. An attentiveness to the Spirit of God in our lives allows us to cut through the fruit of our lives and avoid the worm. It prompts us to unselfish love, of God, and of our neighbour:

> If anyone gives you a cup of water to drink just because you belong to Christ, then I tell you solemnly, he will most certainly not lose his reward (Mk 9:41).

KINGDOM THRESHOLDS

'... so here the Archangel paused
Betwixt the world destroyed and world
  restored...'
          John Milton, *Paradise Lost* (Book 12)

DANTE AND BEATRICE

A Reflection on Christian Love

The story of Dante Alighieri and Beatrice Portinari is one of the most beautiful and enchanting love stories from medieval history. It's the story of a young poet and his unrequited love for a beautiful Florentine girl. They met outside a small church in Florence less than a hundred yards from where Dante was born in 1265. Despite the fact that Dante was only nine years old and Beatrice eight, it was from this first encounter with Beatrice that Dante traced his burning love for her. His *La Vita Nouva* is a collection of poems celebrating his love for Beatrice.[33] It was this love that led Dante on a powerful spiritual pilgrimage that found eventual expression in one of the most beautiful works of medieval history, *The Divine Comedy*, referred to by some as the Fifth Gospel.[34] Although Beatrice enchanted Dante so much, his love for her was unrequited and when Beatrice died in 1290 aged twenty-five Dante spent the rest of his life searching for the origins of love. What was it about his love for Beatrice that seemed to consume his very soul? Was it just about Beatrice or was it a sign of something else, something beyond human love, something beyond even Beatrice herself? Was it a sign of the very love of God himself, the revelation of some prospect that lies ahead, for Dante the prospect of salvation? In the end Dante explained his boyhood encounter with the little girl Beatrice as a moment of profound grace. He saw the love that she kindled in his heart as a reflection of a love that transcended the limits of this world. Just before he died in 1321 Dante completed *The Divine Comedy*. Having been guided through Hell by the Roman poet Virgil and then through Purgatory, finally Dante is led through Paradise, this time by Beatrice. Dante, at least in his writing, had found salvation in the little girl he first saw outside a church door in Florence.

On my first trip to Florence I visited a thirteenth-century building, the reputed home of Dante, and now a museum dedicated to the poet's life and work. On my way back from Dante's house to the main piazza in Florence I came across the *Santa Margherita de' Cerchi*, the church outside of which Dante first saw Beatrice. Just above the heavy wooden door on the outside of the church was a painting of the young poet meeting the young Beatrice. I found myself being quite moved by being there, almost as though, by standing in the very spot depicted above me in the painting, I too shared that first marvellous encounter. I imagined the young Dante walking the few hundred yards from his home, encountering Beatrice for the first time in the narrow street on which I now stood. What was it about her that captivated a boy of nine and encouraged him later to write some of the most beautiful love poetry of all time? Why did she not return his love? And what must he have felt just seventeen years later when Beatrice died at twenty-five? I was surprised to find that there was no one inside the church. It was dark except for the candles that burned, and quiet except for the Gregorian chant that played from a CD player. I lit a candle for Dante and Beatrice and then knelt down on an old wooden kneeler to pray. It took a few minutes to work out the name of the tomb in front of me because of the darkness, but there it was, the tomb of a twenty-five-year-old Florentine girl, Beatrice Portinari. Suddenly I welled up inside and felt something of what Dante might have felt on hearing the news of her death, of what he must have felt years later as he knelt on this same spot. The painting that hung outside, the narrow street, and the tomb of Beatrice had all brought a medieval story of a poet and a young girl suddenly to life.

If I was to present an image or a vision of what Christian love is about then I feel it's to be found in that love story of Dante and Beatrice. The love between two people is a great grace in itself but it is also a kind of revelation of Divine love that transcends the limits and frailties of even the best intentions of human love. Human love is not enough, it falls short of something, it offers us a prospect of something else, a prospect of complete fulfilment in the presence of God's love; in the end, it offers us the prospect of salvation. John's gospel reminds us that our love for each other is a reflection of God's immense love for us:

> As the Father has loved me,
> so I have loved you.
> Remain in my love.
> If you keep my commandments
> you will remain in my love,
> just as I have kept my Father's commandments
> and remain in his love.
> I have told you this
> so that my own joy may be in you
> and your joy be complete (Jn 15: 9-11).

In Dante's love for Beatrice he saw a glimpse of the transcendent, an awareness of a love even more profound. Human love allows us to touch the fringes of God's love, it makes it tangible, something we can experience in the present but which we continue to hope for in the future. When Dante meets Beatrice in Paradise she welcomes him to a place: '...full of love; love of the true good, full of happiness; happiness which transcends any sweetness.'[35]

BEETHOVEN'S CONCERTO

The Twelfth Sunday in Ordinary Time, Year A

Elie Wiesel was sent as a child to the Nazi death camps of Auschwitz and Buchenwald. In 1958, as a young adult, he published *Night*, the story of a child's perceptions of man's inhumanity to man. It's a powerful book that is often disturbing, sometimes hopeful, but always deeply moving because it depicts a world of cruelty. In it Wiesel tells the story of his Polish friend Juliek who refused, above all else, to give up his spirit. He tells how once Juliek and himself were thrown into a darkened shed, full of people, some of whom had been dead for days, others who gasped for breath among the stench of corpses. One day in this dreadful hell, Wiesel could hear the sound of a violin. He wondered what madman could be playing the violin so close to his own death. He thought that it must be Juliek, his Polish friend, who played a fragment from Beethoven's concerto. He wrote how Juliek played such beautiful music as if his soul were the bow, as if his whole life was gliding on the strings of this violin, his lost hopes and his extinguished future. Wiesel talked of how many years later when he heard Beethoven being played, he closed his eyes and thought of the sad, pale face of his Polish friend Juliek, who said farewell on his violin to an audience of dying men. He tried to recall how long Juliek had played for; he must have been overcome with sleep because he woke in the daylight to find the dead body of Juliek slumped over and near him his smashed and trampled violin, '...a strange overwhelming little corpse'[36].

In Jesus' instruction to the Twelve he reminded them:

> Do not be afraid of those who kill the body but cannot kill the soul; fear him rather who can destroy both body and soul in hell. Can you not buy two sparrows for a penny? And yet not one falls to the ground without your Father knowing. Why, every hair on your head has been counted. So there is no need to be afraid; you are worth more than hundreds of sparrows (Mt 10: 28-31).

In every violent society there are remarkable stories of soul courage in the face of death. The Protestant man gripping the hand of a Catholic man who feared that he was going to be shot by Protestant paramilitaries when lined up outside a minibus in January 1976. That little but profound gesture is soul courage in the face of death. It is a reminder, as Seamus Heaney remarked in his Nobel lecture in 1995, that we must make space for the marvellous as well as the murderous.[37] Most of us, of course, are not faced with that life and death dilemma but we are called through our baptism to be prophetic witnesses to the sanctity and dignity of every human life. In a world where the sacredness of human life is constantly under threat it remains our most important Christian vocation to celebrate and defend all of human life. Only by such a profound regard for the human person can we hope, as a Christian people, to regard every human being as made in the image of God, who has counted the very hairs of our heads. Like the Lord of Hosts in Jeremiah we must 'probe with justice' (Jer 20: 12) and seek to create a society where every human life is valued. Paul in his letter to the Romans talks about the gift of divine grace considerably outweighing the fall of sin:

Adam prefigured the One to come, but the gift itself considerably outweighed the fall. If it is certain that through one man's fall so many died, it is even more certain that divine grace, coming through the one man, Jesus Christ, came to so many as an abundant free gift (Rom 5: 15).

Just as Juliek's violin outweighed the despair of violence, so the murderous must make way for the marvellous.

WATER: BETWEEN LIFE AND DEATH

The Feast of the Baptism of the Lord, Year A*

If a sculptor had been looking for an image from which to fashion a modern Pieta (the mother of Christ cradling the dead body of her son), he or she might have found it in the Asian father wading through water with his dead son in the wake of the tsunami disaster that hit coastal Asia in the New Year of 2005. It was one of the first heart-breaking pictures to be shown after the devastation caused by the tsunami wave. The father waded through water up to his waist with the limp body of his son lying across his two arms. It reminded me of the dead body of Christ lying cold across the arms of his mother. Of course there were hundreds, thousands of other children stretched out across the arms of their parents or stretched out on beaches after the waters broke and delivered their lifeless bodies back. In what was one of the saddest natural disasters of our time, we were told that the water retreated and then turned itself around, chasing innocent children and immersing them in death. The sad irony wasn't lost on those who described the tragedy in terms of 'biblical' proportions.

Against the background of the tsunami tragedy I found it difficult, in the context of baptism, to think about water as life-giving. I thought of avoiding it, of focusing on another symbol or meaning for Christian baptism. I thought that to speak about

---

* *(Broadcast on BBC Radio Ulster during a mass to mark 125ᵗʰ anniversary of St Columb's College, 9 January 2005)*

water might make some kind of mockery of the thousands who lost their lives to it. But I've stayed with it as a symbol because our Christian faith is not something separate from the world in which we live; the symbols that we use are not to be understood outside our human experience but from within it, even when that experience is a tragic one.

When we baptise children there is an intimate link between the waters of Christ's baptism in the Jordan and the water that flowed from the side of Christ at his crucifixion. In other words the life-giving water that marks the beginning of Christ's public ministry is also the water that marked his suffering at the end of his ministry. It's a kind of in-between symbol – in-between life and death, in-between grace and sin, in-between creation and its destruction.

There is another link between the water that flowed from the side of Christ and Christ's command to his disciples after his resurrection that they should:

> Go, therefore, make disciples of all the nations;
> baptise them in the name of the Father, and of the Son, and of the Holy Spirit,
> and teach them to observe all the commands I gave you (Mt 28:19-20).

Water equally becomes the beginning of our own ministry and vocation as a Christian people. It is we who are called, in the words of Isaiah, to be a light to the nations...

> to open the eyes of the blind,
> to free captives from prison,
> and those who live in darkness from the dungeon (Is 42:7).

Local churches and charities were inundated in the aftermath of the tragedy with people asking how they could help those affected by the tsunami. Thousands made very generous financial donations. Somewhere in all of us is that deep desire, that profound sympathy that wants to free those who are living in the darkness of despair, desperation and grief. To become disciples of Christ, to share in his baptism and his mission, that is the deepest meaning of Christ's baptism. That is the Good News that Peter wants to share with Cornelius and his household in Acts:

> Peter addressed them: 'The truth I have now come to realise' he said, 'is that God does not have favourites, but that anybody of any nationality who fears God and does what is right is acceptable to him (Acts 10:34-35).

When our baptism is realised fully in a desire to bring the light of Christ into the darkest corners of people's lives, then water does become life-giving rather than destructive. Water is the medium through which we share in Christ's baptism, his death and resurrection. It becomes a means of hope, a reminder that death and destruction, however seemingly total, do not have the last word. We live as a Christian people between water as a symbol of death and life, destruction and renewal, sadness and hope. As baptised Christians we trust in the God who called us to be his people.

THE CHRISTMAS CHILD

A Christmas Reflection

Christmas is welcomed and dreaded in almost equal measure. That it is the season of goodwill depends on one's point of view. I find celebrating Christmas Day mass difficult because there is a balance to be found that I have come to believe is almost impossible. There are those in the congregation who have been waiting for this day as anxiously and expectantly as their children; there are others who have dreaded it and are hoping that it will be over quickly. No family is without its ups and downs, but for some families Christmas Day is a day of enforced joy, shallow happiness and sore memories. I am talking about people who will celebrate Christmas for the first time without their mother who shared intimately their first memory of Christmas and until now shared every other Christmas Day. I am talking about parents who have lost their child to cancer or in a road accident in the last year, parents whose heart has been ripped from them and for whom Christmas Day is a difficult time. I am talking about children who will suffer neglect or abuse because of a parent's over-indulgence in alcohol at Christmas, whose presents are sullied by the absence of love, the lack of security. I am talking about the man or woman who will spend Christmas Day and night in a homeless shelter, estranged from their families. This all sounds terribly negative but I am conscious that at Christmas Day mass someone who is suffering as a result of one of those situations is present. I am also conscious of the children and parents and others who are there smiling and enjoying the goodwill of Christmas and so they should. Parents who have watched the magic in their children's eyes as they ran down the stairs to see what Santa left; parents who have said sorry to each other for a misunderstanding and made up in the spirit of Christmas; families who are brought together from different parts of the world for this one day in the year. There is so much to celebrate about Christmas too, so much good, so much love. So how do I speak to all those people? What message do I give that might reach across the joy and sadness in those present?

At the heart of Christmas is the Christ child, the Child of Christmas who has something powerful to say to everyone. He is the Child of new birth and anticipated suffering, the Child of warmth and of exile, the Child of welcome and derision. Christ is the child between sadness and joy, hurt and healing, death and life. In offering the people at Christmas Day mass a message, I offer this reflection:

> If you have lost a loved one this year – a child, a parent, a partner, a friend – then Christ the child of consolation is for you. If you have had a newborn child this year then Christ the child of joy is for you;

> If you have become estranged from your family, from those you love because of misunderstanding or mistakes, then Christ the child who was estranged from his parents in the Temple is for you. If you have become reconciled with a loved one, then Christ the healing child is for you;

> If you cannot return to the country of your birth this Christmas because of fear or war, than Christ the child

who fled into Egypt is for you. If you have returned home to your family for Christmas, then Christ the child of welcome is for you;

If you are recovering from an addiction to alcohol or drugs, then Christ the child of strength is for you. If you are despairing of any progress, then Christ the child of hope is for you;

If your heart is troubled by fear or anxiety, then Christ the child of peace is for you. If you are at peace with yourself and others, then Christ the child of gratitude is for you;

If your marriage has broken down then Christ the child of comfort is for you; if you have married someone you love then Christ the child of love is for you;

If you are tired by life and its anxieties then Christ the child of rest is for you; if you are full of expectancy and joy then Christ the child of celebration is for you.

Christ the Christmas child is for all of us in our joys and sorrows, our successes and failures, our fears and our dreams. Christmas, when we welcome the Christ-child, is not just for children.

MICHELANGELO'S SNOWMAN

The First Sunday of Advent, Year B

In one of his poems the modern Irish poet Tony Curtis refers to an apocryphal story about Michelangelo, according to which the most beautiful sculpture he ever made was a snowman in the Boboli Gardens in Florence. Curtis writes how old Italians said it was a male nude chiseled out of ice:

> ...you could see where his soul
> was held. He turned all to tears
> and was washed away.[38]

Whether or not Michelangelo ever did sculpt such a snowman, the story is a beautiful one. It took me back to my childhood and the simple innocence involved in making snowmen after a snowfall. We thought nothing of packing snow for hours and sculpting something, however crude, in the shape of a snowman. In our efforts and our excitement we forgot about the thaw, the inevitable disappearance of our creation, even as we packed it with snow. I do remember a sadness at its thawing, a sense of loss, however small, however insignificant in the scheme of things. That nothing remained, no ruins to suggest a grandeur that once had been, was strange.

I thought of my own and Michelangelo's snowman when I read Isaiah's plea for God to return to his sinful servants:

> You were angry when we were sinners;
> we had long been rebels against you.
> We were all like men unclean,
> all that integrity of ours like filthy clothing.
> We have all withered like leaves
> and our sins blew us away like the wind (Is 64:5-6).

Isaiah uses the image of autumn leaves to suggest our death, our fragile place in the world without God. We are no more permanent than the snowman whose life is cut short even as he is created. Without the love and mercy of God our beauty is for a moment, passing like the autumn leaves or the winter snow. But Isaiah's plea is heard and St Paul, in his letter to the Corinthians, gives thanks to God for the graces received through Jesus Christ. He tells the Corinthians:

> ...the witness to Christ has indeed been strong among you so that you will not be without any of the gifts of the Spirit while you are waiting for our Lord Jesus Christ to be revealed; and he will keep you steady and without blame until the last day, the day of our Lord Jesus Christ, because God by calling you has joined you to his Son, Jesus Christ; and God is faithful (1Cor 1:6-9).

Faith in the God who is faithful makes sense of our passing lives, of our place in the world as pilgrims, passing through this life. The prospect that there is nothing after we die, no trace of the person that we once had been, fills us with an emptiness, a sadness even as we live. It is in our nature to look for permanence, to pursue something more, something beyond us, something after this mortal life. It is our faith that rescues us from despair, from desperation. We place our mortal lives in the context of the eternal life promised to us by God and we act as pilgrims in this passing world, ready for the master to knock and find us awake.

There are temptations, of course, to look for permanence here and now, to make of this world's passing pleasures something more, an end in themselves rather than a spur to final contentment with God. We live our lives, sometimes, as if they were permanent, as if the master will not return. We need to remind ourselves of our place here, as guests passing on to somewhere else. Advent is a time for reflection on why we are here and where we are going. The readings are full of expectancy, a sense of urgency, of a call towards repentance. We are called to be vigilant, to awaken from our spiritual slumber:

> So stay awake, because you do not know when the master of the house is coming, evening, midnight, cockcrow, dawn; if he comes unexpectedly, he must not find you asleep. And what I say to you I say to all: Stay awake! (Mk 13:35-37).

Trusting in God's goodness we know that we will not wither away like Isaiah's leaves or melt away like Michelangelo's snowman.

THE GIFT OF THE EUCHARIST

The Tenth Sunday in Ordinary Time, Year A

One of the saddest moments of my priesthood was an encounter I had with a middle-aged woman in Derry. I was in town when I met a friend of mine and we began to talk. As we spoke I noticed a woman, in tears, walking past us. She said hello to me as she went past. As she walked away she would occasionally stop and look back as if she wanted to speak to me but somehow couldn't. I became increasingly uncomfortable wondering if she had received bad news. There was something terribly desperate about having to carry such news on her own. I said goodbye to my friend and walked out onto the street, hoping to catch up with her. When I did, I asked her if there was anything I could do to help. Still crying, she told me about her brother and how he suffered from alcoholism. He had stopped drinking for a while but had now begun binge drinking and was in a desperate state. She told me that he was a good man but was reckless with alcohol. She was crying, she said, because she needed someone to talk to. I will always remember what she said because of the sense of shame I felt. 'I have no right to be talking to you Father', she said, 'because I broke the rules of the Church. I'm divorced and I don't go to Mass anymore... I would like to but I would feel a hypocrite... I'm sorry but I really shouldn't be wasting your time'. I felt a sense of shame because somewhere, at some time, the

Church had failed to communicate to this woman the compassion, love and mercy of Jesus Christ. I tried to say this, to say that all of us in life make mistakes but that God's love is bigger than any human institution and more embracing than any human failure. I spoke of Christ's love for her, of his desire to welcome her back but I couldn't help but feel that in a single moment I was trying to undo twenty-four years of shame, guilt and a sense of exclusion from the Church. When I left her I felt hugely disappointed at my own weakness, her sense of isolation and our church's failure to convey to this woman the humanity of Jesus Christ.

I doubt if this woman was ever told explicitly that she was not welcome to attend Sunday Mass. However, her experience of the church was one of exclusion and isolation and it is enough that a person feels that sense of isolation strongly to make it very real and damaging for them. It is a very real problem for today's Church: how do we address that sense of exclusion that a significant number of faithful people experience? How do we make the Church less exclusive and more inclusive? How do we address the sense that many people have of being excluded from receiving the Eucharist for one reason or another? I believe that these are fundamental questions for the life of the Church today. In the last decade the experience of the Irish Church has taught us that there is no great divide between the sinners and the virtuous. All of us, priests and people, live between grace and failure. All of us are in desperate need of the grace of God, the forgiveness of Jesus Christ and the guidance and inspiration of the Holy Spirit. The love of God for his people and the mercy and forgiveness of Jesus Christ are at the very heart of two bible passages, one from Hosea and the other from Matthew's gospel. The twin theme in both readings is God's desire for love and mercy, not sacrifice and holocausts. In the passage from Hosea we read:

This love of yours is like a morning cloud, like the dew that quickly disappears. This is why I have torn them to pieces by the prophets, why I slaughtered them with the words from my mouth, since what I want is love, not sacrifice; knowledge of God, not holocausts (Hos 6:4-6).

Matthew addresses the theme of mercy in his gospel story:

While he was at dinner in the house it happened that a number of tax collectors and sinners came to sit at the table with Jesus and his disciples. When the Pharisees saw this, they said to his disciples, 'Why does your master eat with tax collectors and sinners?' When he heard this he replied, 'It is not the healthy who need the doctor, but the sick. Go and learn the meaning of the words: What I want is mercy, not sacrifice. And indeed I did not come to call the virtuous, but sinners (Mt 9:10-13).

We can no longer afford the luxury as priests, if ever we thought we could, of instilling in some of our faithful people a sense of exclusion. The sad lessons of the last decade may even yet turn terrible hurt to some good if we become a more humble, inclusive and compassionate Church. All is grace.

DAVID AND THE SLAVES

The Easter Vigil

Nothing could have prepared me for the monumental presence and beauty of Michelangelo's *David* in the Accademia Gallery in Florence. Michelangelo sculpted the young David, the future King of Israel, from a single block of marble between 1501 and 1504. The *David* stands in the centre of a large room designed like a Latin cross-shaped church. I had always imagined a single, circular room with *David* as the only occupant casting his determined expression over his many thousand admirers. While *David*'s physical presence and his familiarity as one of the world's most famous pieces of sculpture ensures his place of pride towards the end of the long room, he is not alone. He stands, rather, at the end of a room known as The Gallery of Slaves, visited by almost one million tourists each year.

David's place in the room is well chosen; visitors to the gallery enter the room by a door furthest away from and directly opposite him. It is the first room in the gallery and the sight of *David* so soon is sudden and somewhat overwhelming. I was impressed by his physical beauty, his presence and his creator's perfect sense of proportion. I felt a profound sense of gratitude to Michelangelo, a sense of sharing in something beyond me, a sense of beauty beyond myself. I tried to see myself in this glorified body, to find the twisted timber of my humanity in this profound expression of beauty. A sign on the stone pediment on which he stood read 'Do not touch'; fair enough, I thought, for something so beautiful might turn to dust.

I found myself much more at home in The Gallery of the Slaves, in the sense that I could relate to Michelangelo's contorted figures of humanity. Among the unfinished sculptures on each side of this long room are four sculptures originally intended to decorate the tomb of Pope Julius II. Burdened with the weight of their own stone each slave struggles to free himself from the marble that weighs him down. In contrast to the perfect form of the David these sculptures twist and turn in their struggle for freedom, freedom from the very stone that defines them. One slave appears to be carrying a huge weight of stone on his head; however, the weight is the unfinished head itself, the uncut stone. The slave is known as *Atlas,* after the Titan in Greek mythology who is punished for his part in the revolt of the Titans by having to carry the weight of the sky on his head. For all the crude chisel marks and imprisoned figures, I found the slaves profoundly moving. I could identify people I have met in my ministry in that stone; I have seen people enslaved in the stone of their past, unable to free themselves from their own weight; I have seen the chisel marks of pain on the faces of many good people. Suddenly I understood something of the Easter experience in that room in Florence and of Paul's letter to the Romans:

> You have been taught that when we were baptised in Christ Jesus we were baptised in his death; in other words, when we were baptised we went into the tomb with him and joined him in death, so that as Christ was raised from the dead by the Father's glory, we too might live a new life.

> If in union with Christ we have imitated his death, we shall also imitate his resurrection. We must realise that

our former selves have been crucified with him to destroy this sinful body and to free us from the slavery of sin. When a man dies, of course, he has finished with sin (Rom 6:3-7).

The Easter Vigil celebrates the wonderful story of our redemption from the moment of our creation to our faithlessness and redemption through Christ's death and resurrection. Paul uses the analogy of slavery, a familiar custom in the ancient world, to explain our tendency to sin. Slavery binds us and weighs us down in the same way that Michelangelo's slaves cannot free themselves from their own weight. The Easter joy that we celebrate, however, is that Christ has freed us from our sins through his death and that we shall share his glory 'when Christ will raise our mortal bodies and make them like his own in glory' (Eucharistic Prayer III). Christ's disciples failed to recognise him on the road to Emmaus:

> two of them were on their way to a village called Emmaus, seven miles from Jerusalem, and they were talking together about all that had happened. Now as they talked this over, Jesus himself came up and walked by their side; but something prevented them from recognising him (Lk 24:13-16).

The appearance of Christ had changed so much that the disciples only recognise him at the breaking of the bread. We too believe that we will share Christ's glory at the end of time. Michelangelo's slaves speak eloquently of our human condition weighed down by sin; his David points to our final redemption when Christ will come again in his glory.

THE TEARS OF ST PETER

The Second Sunday in Ordinary Time, Year A

The Tears of St Peter is one of the most moving paintings of the apostle to whom Christ gave the keys of the kingdom. It was painted by the sixteenth-century artist El Greco, originally from the Greek island of Crete but who settled in Toledo, Spain. Apparently he was a devout man who was keen to tell the sacred stories in a new and stirring manner. His paintings are almost mystical in their bold design and dramatic vision. *The Tears of St Peter* is no less bold and dramatic. El Greco paints the moment after Christ's arrest, when St Peter, upon hearing a cock crow, realised that he had fulfilled Christ's prophecy and denied him three times. The weather in the painting is bleak and in turmoil, mirroring the state of St Peter's mind. Tears sit heavy on his eyes as he looks up towards heaven in desperation and remorse. Peter has been unfaithful in his vocation. The denial of Christ is his lowest moment.

There is another story told about Peter in the apocryphal Acts of Peter. The story alleges that Peter, fleeing his martyrdom in Rome, meets Christ on the road. He asked Christ, *'Domine, quo vadis?'*, 'Lord, where are you going?' and Christ answered, 'To Rome, to be crucified again.' The story goes that Peter, reassured by Christ, overcame his fear of martyrdom and returned to Rome to face his executioners. Whether or not the story is true, it resonates with the Peter we know from the gospels, someone who is afraid and confused, but always obedient in the end.

I like Peter; I find him authentic in his fear, his denial and in the end in his acceptance of his vocation and his obedience to Christ. All of us of who follow Christ are called to the same obedience and we are asked to imitate the obedience of Christ to the will of his Father, an obedience celebrated in God's approval of his Son:

> John also declared, 'I saw the Spirit coming down on him from heaven like a dove and resting on him. I did not know him myself, but he who sent me to baptise with water had said to me, "The man on whom you see the Spirit come down and rest is the one who is going to baptize with the Holy Spirit." Yes, I have seen and I am the witness that he is the Chosen One of God' (Jn 1:32-34).

In imitation of Christ, all of us are called, like the people of Corinth, to take our place 'among all the saints everywhere who pray to our Lord Jesus Christ' (1Cor 1:2). Obedience is difficult, particularly in the culture in which we live. It is viewed by many as an outdated virtue, something akin to slavery or exploitation. We live in a culture of rights and individual freedom where limits to that freedom are often viewed as repressive and claustrophobic. In the context of that kind of culture it might be difficult to appreciate Isaiah's remark that he was formed in the womb to be the Lord's servant (49:5), the idea that even before we are born God has a plan for each of us, a plan to be understood, only in obedience to him. Like Peter we struggle between denial and witness, between faithfulness and betrayal. Christianity is a difficult vocation; it calls us to obedience, to service of others, to forgiveness, and often to suffering. There are modern witnesses today, like Peter, who suffer their own personal martyrdom and yet remain faithful to Christ. There are good people who lose loved ones, good parents who lose children, good children who lose parents. Life is hard for many people and they clutch to their faith to save themselves from drowning. Like Peter they cry to the heavens in desperation, their eyes filled with sadness and grief. But even in their clutching, because of their clutching, they are faithful people.

The tears that Peter shed in his struggle to come to terms with his faith and his vocation are shared by many, if not all, who are sincere in living out the Christian life. Sometimes when I speak to people and I ask them how they are it's as if suddenly their pain wells up inside them and spills out in signs of deep hurt and pain. People carry terrible weights, weights of regret, of failure, of deep pain from a past hurt. Peter is their saint, our saint, those of us who live our lives between dread and witness, faithfulness and fear, sin and grace.

CHRIST THE TEACHER

The Fourth Sunday in Ordinary Time, Year A (Catechetical Sunday)

In summertime, as a child, I got up after nine and walked with my grandmother down to St Eugene's Cathedral for 10 o'clock mass. I remember those days as some of the happiest of my life. There wasn't just mass of course, but a whole ritual that surrounded it. I had to bless myself passing the church and take my hands out of my pockets before I went inside. I had to dip my finger in one of the two stone water fonts that were built into the wall of the porch opposite each other. My grandmother used to kiss the feet of the marble Christ that stood inside the door on the left and I did the same. I never really understood why and I never asked; it was part of a ritual that must have meant something, otherwise my grandmother wouldn't have done it. Then there were rules during mass. I bowed my head when the name Jesus was mentioned. I stayed on my knees after receiving holy communion until I stood up for the final blessing of the mass. Then there were the Stations of the Cross and more kissing of statues. And then, every summer morning, we walked down to the local shop, bought a fruit malt loaf and ate it between us when we came home.

I wasn't exactly sure then, as a boy of eight, what was going on; and I wonder as I reflect back to those summers if my grandmother could have articulated what it was all about. But now that I look back, I see a whole pattern emerging, something happening almost beyond the daily ritual that we shared. Twenty-five years on I find myself making the sign of the cross at every church I pass, touching the feet of statues when I enter a church, and frowning to myself when I watch people stand casually at the back of a church with their hands in their pockets.

But now at thirty-three I remember something more than the mass, and the rituals, something else shared on the walk down and up the hill called Academy Road. One hundred and twenty-five people lost their lives in the Troubles in 1979. Pope John Paul II made a plea for an end to the conflict when he visited Ireland. I remember my grandmother talking about that; I remember her sadness at the death of anyone in the Troubles. When she was a young woman she lost three children of her own because of sickness, one after the other. She knew what suffering was about, what it was to grieve, to lose someone you loved. I remember days when people were killed – soldiers, policemen and women, paramilitaries and civilians – my grandmother used to ask me to pray for their families at mass. She hated politics and bigotry and she had it drummed in to me that all of us would have to face God at the end for our judgement. It was on the hill of Academy Road that my grandmother taught me about mercy, about peacemakers, about those who mourn.

> Seeing the crowds, he [Jesus] went up the hill. There he sat down and was joined by his disciples. Then he began to speak. This is what he taught them:
> 'How happy are the poor in spirit;
> theirs is the kingdom of heaven.
> Happy the gentle:
> they shall have the earth for their heritage.
> Happy those who mourn:
> they shall be comforted.
> Happy those who hunger and thirst for what is right:
> they shall be satisfied.

Happy the merciful:
they shall have mercy shown them.
Happy the poor in heart:
they shall see God.
Happy the peacemakers:
they shall be called sons of God.
Happy those who are persecuted in the cause of right:
theirs is the kingdom of heaven' (Mt 5: 3-10).

As grateful as I am to the two schools that educated me as a young boy and as a teenager, the education that I learned from those summer days, when school was over, has shaped how I see the world. The seed of my vocation to the priesthood was sown in those days and my understanding of the dignity of every human person was learned from that first teacher. No teacher, however wise or inspiring, will ever be able to replace the wisdom of a loving committed parent or grandparent.

THE KISS OF CHRIST

The First Sunday of Lent, Year C

The story of *The Grand Inquisitor* is one of the most remarkable and incisive pieces of writing by the nineteenth-century Russian writer Dostoyevsky. The context is a 'poem', written by the revolutionary Ivan, and read to his brother Alexey, a religious novice. The action of the poem is set in Seville in Spain during the Inquisition. Christ decides to visit his people briefly, to walk among them again 'with a gentle smile of infinite compassion.'[39] People recognise him instantly and he heals a blind man and raises a little girl of seven from death. Just at the moment that the little girl rises out of her coffin, the Cardinal, the Grand Inquisitor passes by the cathedral in the square. He is an old man of nearly ninety and as he watches the spectacle before him he orders his guards to seize Christ. So submissive are the people to his power and authority that they make way for his guards and allow Christ to be taken. As night falls, the old Cardinal begins his interrogation of Christ in a darkened cell. He insists that Christ has no right to add anything to what he said fifteen hundred years ago. Christ gave people freedom but they couldn't cope with it and so they humbly laid it at the feet of the Church. The Cardinal then goes on to remind Christ of the three temptations in the desert. He says that Christ refused to turn stones into loaves of bread because he didn't want to buy man's freedom with bread. But the

Inquisitor reminds him that bread from heaven cannot compare with earthly bread and that millions will not have the strength to give up earthly bread to follow Christ in freedom. Men are by nature weak and rebellious but in the end they will be obedient to the Church. Christ should have given them earthly bread and then they would have worshipped him. 'Without a clear idea of what to live for, man will not consent to live and will rather destroy himself than remain on the earth, though he were surrounded by loaves of bread.'[40]

The Cardinal moves on to the second temptation of Christ which was to throw himself down from a great height and trust in the angels of God to save him. In rejecting a miracle, the Cardinal suggests, Christ again did not understand that without a miracle men would refuse to believe in God. In refusing to come down from the cross Christ hungered for a faith based on free will and not on miracles. The Inquisitor rebukes his prisoner – 'You hungered for freely given love and not for the servile raptures of the slave before the might that has terrified him once and for all. But here, too, your judgement of men was too high, for they are slaves, though rebels by nature.'[41] The Cardinal tells Christ that the Church has corrected his work and has based it instead on 'miracle, mystery, and authority.'

Finally he turns to the last temptation, the offer to Christ of all the kingdoms in the world, the offer, the Cardinal argues, that would have united mankind in a single conscience, with one individual to worship, in universal peace. It is the Church who has taken the 'sword of Caesar' and rejected Christ. 'With us, however, all will be happy and will no longer rise in rebellion or exterminate one another, as they do everywhere under your freedom. Oh, we will convince them that only then will they become free when they have resigned their freedom to us and have submitted to us.'[42]

The *Grand Inquisitor* is to be understood in the context of Dostoyevsky's *The Brothers Karamazov* which deals with questions of belief in God and atheism. But even in that context it touches on something about the nature of free will in a deep way. The 'poem' sets up Christ and his gift of freedom against the weakness and herd mentality of the multitude. There is a logic to what the Cardinal says; freedom weighs heavily on people and greater obedience to Christ might have been secured by feeding people's earthly hunger, their desire for miracles and for unity. The whole monologue is best summed up in the Cardinal's question, 'Why is the weak soul to blame for being unable to receive gifts so terrible?'[43] In other words, did Christ overestimate mankind, in Dostoyevsky's story, in dying for them so that in freedom they could accept him? Surely Christ had burdened people with freedom of choice, a freedom that was beyond them, a freedom that is beyond us?

Are we the same as the multitudes in the story who slavishly laid down their freedom at the feet of a higher earthly authority, rather than follow Christ in freedom and in truth? Did Christ overestimate their capacity to love in freedom and follow him in faith? Does Christ overestimate our ability to choose to love him and our brothers and sisters in freedom and in the context of a faith not based on miracles? The answer of course lies in Christ's redeeming love for us, which through grace, means that we are no longer slaves but brothers and sisters in Jesus Christ. Christ's death has freed us from slavery so that we are no longer weak, rebellious souls, but disciples of Christ sharing in his redemptive work. Christ's love, expressed most fully on the cross, burns within us and redeems us. At the end of The Grand Inquisitor the Cardinal is distressed by the prisoner's silence. He wants him to say something, however bitter. But instead Christ approaches the old man and kisses him on his 'bloodless, ageless lips'. Startled he opens the prison door and releases the prisoner telling him never to come again. Alexey asks his brother about the old Cardinal? Ivan replies, 'The kiss glows in his heart, but the old man sticks to his idea.'[44]

Like the souls in Dostoyevsky's story, we are at times weak, rebellious and vulnerable and lured by the attractions of this world and the security they bring. We are tempted to stick to our ideas, ideas of happiness, of fulfillment, of ourselves as the makers of our own destiny. But all of us have been kissed by Christ and redeemed by him. We are not slaves condemned to live out our lives pursuing fulfillment in earthly goods, wealth and power. There are moments in our fragile lives of faith when we are asked to stop and re-examine our ideas. Lent, especially, is a time when we are encouraged to look at ourselves, to reflect on the freedom Christ has won for us and above all to ponder, in our hearts, his kiss.

NOTES

1. Edited and annotated by A. Norman Jeffares, *Yeats's Poems*, (Papermac, 1989) pp.294-5

2. William Trevor, *A Bit on the Side*, (Penguin, 2004) p.40

3. Ian McEwan, *Saturday*, Quality Paperbacks Direct, 2005

4. *Yeats's Poems*, op.cit, p.53

5. See W.R.F. Browning, *A Dictionary of the Bible*, (Oxford University Press, 1996) p.322

6. Louis McNeice, *Selected Poems*, (Faber and Faber, 1998), p.xv

7. Quoted in *A Rage for Order, Poetry of the Northern Ireland Troubles*, Ed. Frank Ormsby (Blackstaff Press, 1992) p.79

8. Fyodor Dostoyevsky, *The Brothers Karamazov*, translated by David Magarshack, (Penguin 1958) p.287

9. Karl Rahner, *On Prayer* (The Liturgical Press, Collegeville Minnesota, 1993) p.59

10. Quoted in *The Strength of Poetry* by James Fenton (Oxford, 2001) p.85

11. Quoted in *Scanning the Century, The Penguin Book of the Twentieth Century in Poetry*, Ed. Peter Forbes (Viking, 1999) p.341

12. *Lost Lives – The stories of the men, women and children who died as a result of the Northern Ireland troubles*, edited by David McKittrick, Seamus Kelters, Brian Feeney and Chris Thornton (Mainstream Publishing Company, 1999).

13. Hannah Arendt, *Eichmann in Jerusalem: A Report on the Banality of Evil* (New York, Viking Press, 1963).

14. Brian Friel, *Selected Stories* (Gallery Press, 1979) p.15

15. Kate Clanchey, *Newborn* (Picador, 2004) pp.1-2

16. Nicholas Boyle, *Sacred and Secular Scriptures – A Catholic Approach to Literature*, (Darton, Longman and Todd, 2004) p.70

17. Graham Greene, *The Power and the Glory*, (Penguin Books, 1962) p.60

18. Alexander Solzhenitsyn, *One Word of Truth:* The Nobel Speech on Literature, London, 1970
19. See *The Beauty of Christ, An Introduction to the Theology of Hans Urs von Balthasar,* edited by Bede McGregor, OP and Thomas Norris, (T&T Clark Ltd, 1994).
20. Ernst H. Gombrich, *The Story of Art,* (Phaidon Press Limited, 1995) p.393
21. George Steiner, *Grammars of Creation,* (Faber and Faber, 2001) p.72
22. Quoted in Tom Stack *No Earthly Estate, God and Patrick Kavanagh: An Anthology,* (Columba Press, 2002) p.47
23. *Cana Revisited,* quoted in *Door into the Dark,* (Faber & Faber, 1969) p.18
24. Jonathon Sacks, *The Politics of Hope,* (Jonathan Cape, 1997) pp. 191, 195
25. See Johann Christoph Arnold's *The Lost Art of Forgiving – Stories of healing from the cancer of bitterness,* (The Plough Publishing House, 1998).
26. Seamus Heaney, *The Cure at Troy,* (Faber and Faber, 1990) p.77
27. Homer, *The Iliad,* translated with an introduction by Martin Hammond, (Penguin, 1987) Book XXIV
28. Michael Longley, *Selected Poems,* (Cape Poetry, 1998) p.118
29. Iris Murdoch, *The Bell,* (Penguin, 1958) p.235
30. See *The Image of Christ – The Catalogue of the exhibition Seeing Salvation,* (National Gallery Company Ltd, 2000)
31. Brian Moore, *Lies of Silence,* (Vintage Paperbacks, 1990)
32. James Wood, *The Book Against God,* (Jonathan Cape, 2003) p.247
33. Dante Alighieri, *La Vita Nouva,* (Penguin, 2004)
34. Dante Alighieri, *The Divine Comedy,* (Oxford World's Classics, 1998)
35. Ibid. *Paradiso* XXX, lines 42-3
36. Elie Wiesel, *Night,* (Penguin, 1981) p.107
37. Seamus Heaney, *Crediting Poetry,* (Gallery Books, 1995) p.20
38. *What Darkness Covers,* quoted in *Poetry Ireland Review,* edited by Maurice Harmon, issue 70, Autumn 2001, pp.5-6
39. Fyodor Dostoyevsky, *The Brothers Karamazov,* translated by David Magarshack, (Penguin Books, 1958) p.291
40. Ibid. p.298
41. Ibid. p.300
42. bid. p.303
43. Ibid. p.301
44. Ibid. p.30